The Retirement Pitfall

Retirement Mistakes
The Government Never Told You About

Bill is always Right!!

Simon Chu

outskirts press
DENVER, COLORADO

The opinions expressed in this manuscript are solely the opinions of the author and do not represent the opinions or thoughts of the publisher. The author has represented and warranted full ownership and/or legal right to publish all the materials in this book.

The Retirement Pitfall
Retirement Mistakes The Government Never Told You About
All Rights Reserved.
Copyright © 2013 Simon Chu
V2.0 R1.1

Cover by Simon Chu

This book may not be reproduced, transmitted, or stored in whole or in part by any means, including graphic, electronic, or mechanical without the express written consent of the publisher except in the case of brief quotations embodied in critical articles and reviews.

Outskirts Press, Inc.
http://www.outskirtspress.com

ISBN: 978-1-4787-1461-3

Outskirts Press and the "OP" logo are trademarks belonging to Outskirts Press, Inc.

PRINTED IN THE UNITED STATES OF AMERICA

Many books have been written about how to properly plan for retirement, but they always assume that the retirement planning began when you are young. This book is for people who are approaching retirement or are in retirement that gives them the tools to help them reach success regardless of their financial history. It's never too late to plan for retirement. Even if you are older and don't have a plan, there are ways to catch up. From avoiding common mistakes and controlling your spending, to financial planning and constructing your estate, Simon teaches you to build a retirement plan designed to weather any storm.

Disclaimer

FINANCIAL PLANNING IS challenging. It becomes more challenging as you begin to factor in things such as individual wants and desires. This is compounded by variables such as unique personal circumstances and ever-changing regulations. This book is meant to explain common scenarios and financial planning given the best practices. The hypothetical examples given in this book are for illustrative purposes only. Returns are not indicative of any particular investment. Unless specifically stated otherwise, examples assume reinvestment of dividends with no consequence of fees or taxes. Keep in mind that investments will fluctuate with changes in market conditions. This book in no way discusses all options available to investors. It reflects my opinion, and is subject to my limitations. These opinions are not intended to provide specific advice and should not be construed as recommendations for any individual. This book is published with the understanding that the author is not engaged in rendering legal or tax services. While designed to provide accurate information on retirement plan distributions, the services of competent law and tax professionals should be sought prior to executing any strategy. Investments involve risk including the potential for loss of the principal amount invested. Please remember that investment decisions should be based on an individual's goals, time horizon, and tolerance for risk.

Contents

I. Introduction 1
II. Chapter 1 – Common Fears and Questions 9
- Borrow and You Shall Receive
- A House of Straw
- Present Day
- The Overall Economy
- Is Retirement Obsolete?
- Get Back In There
- Preparing for Retirement
- Approaching Retirement – What Can Be Done?

III. Chapter 2 – Common Mistakes 31
- Fear… Again
- Do You Have a Plan?
- Do You Have Proper Advice?
- How to Find a Good Advisor
- Are You Making Excuses?
- Your Home is Not an Asset
- Dealing With Family
- Other Common Mistakes

IV. Chapter 3 – Spending / Old Habits 54
- Money Is Emotional
- Money's Understudy

- In For a Penny, In For a Pound
- Inheritances
- How Can You Improve Your Bad Spending Habits?

V. Chapter 4 – Investments 71
- Stay cool
- Know Your Objectives
- Securities
- Managing Your investments
- Knowing When to Buy and sell
- Inflation
- Investing for income

VI. Chapter 5 – Financial Planning for Retirement 91
- Step 1: Determine What You Have and What You Want
- Step 2: How Will You Get There?
- Step 3: Preparing For the Unknown
- Step 4: Stay Flexible
- Be Investment Smart

VII. Chapter 6 – Social Security 106
- The Basics
- The Math
- Love and Marriage
- Work and Income
- Tax
- Changing Your Benefits
- Medicare

VIII. Chapter 7 – Retirement Plans / IRAs 125
- 401(k)s
- The IRA
- Rollovers
- Withdrawals
- Stretch IRA
- Roth IRA

IX.	Chapter 8 – Insurance In Retirement................	158
	• Life Insurance	
	• Long Term Care	
X.	Chapter 9 – Estate Planning	176
	• What is Estate Planning?	
	• What Do You Have?	
	• Common Estate Plans	
	• Other Estate Planning Options	
	• Making a Good Plan	
XI.	Epilogue..	199
XII.	About the Author	201

Introduction

IN MY MANY years as a financial advisor I have been asked countless questions about what it takes to have a successful and secure retirement. "What are safe investments for someone like me? How much money should I have for a comfortable retirement? How can I secure my possessions and prevent taxes from the government?" And more recently "How can I hope to retire after The Great Recession?"

There is plenty of advice for people about how to plan a retirement. Just Google the word "Retirement" and you will be inundated with articles that help you plan for retirement or prepare for retirement. There is so much information out there on the topic it can be overwhelming. The problem is all of these articles presuppose that you are some 20 or 30-something, thinking long-term, and sitting atop your pile of money just waiting to invest. You and I both know that this situation is the exception and not the rule. Unfortunately, many people do not begin really taking action for their retirement until much later. Sometimes they did not save because they needed the money when they were younger, and sometimes they simply did not save because of bad habits like overspending or procrastination. The fact is that much of the information about retirement is just not applicable to most people, not because it is bad advice, but simply because it is not what people are looking for when they begin looking for answers about retirement. Of course, investing for retirement

THE RETIREMENT PITFALL

early is an excellent strategy, but when I read that in every article I come across I almost want to say "Well, DUH! Tell me something I don't know!" While early retirement planning is something that will be talked about for a full understanding of the retirement process, the important thing that this book will tell you is how to plan in your later years. This book will explain retirement planning for retirees.

You may not have invested prudently for your retirement, but that does not mean that you are now some sort of financial pariah. There are still things that you can do immediately before retirement and during retirement that can mean the difference between success and comfort for you and your loved ones, or waiting desperately for that Social Security check in the mail. If you did save for retirement and have a good nest egg in the works, that is fantastic! However, now is not the time to rest on your laurels. As Shelley once said "Nothing wilts faster than laurels that have been rested upon". If you manage and maintain that investment it can give you options and independence you previously thought not possible and improve any legacy you leave your children or grandchildren.

The reason I want to help people take steps to enjoy their retirement is because, as a young boy, I saw firsthand the dangers of relying on others in your later years. I was born to a middle class family. My mother and my father were both engineers and education was seen as the most important indicator of success in my family. Good grades meant good child. What was taught in school and at home was that you do well in school, work hard, go to college, and get a good paying job working as an employee. Little thought was given to the idea of planning for retirement. It was assumed that you should work hard during your years of employment and your company would take care of the rest. But the company did not take care of "the rest". It was difficult to watch as my parents moved into retirement with only a little savings and the promise of support from their former employer. After they realized the promises made to them were not what they seemed, the options to them were limited. Either continue working for the rest of their lives, or rely on the government to see them through

INTRODUCTION

their golden years. I felt that as elders of the family and community my parents deserved to live with comfort and respect. This experience showed me that many people need help in finding their way to a retirement where they themselves can be satisfied. I resolved that people should not have to live this way and I needed to do something about it. I realized that everyone needed to become wise in the ways of finance and that I could show them the path to living the way they had imagined.

This story is similar for many families in America. Instead of saving for retirement themselves, most Americans of our parents' generation relied on their jobs for the promise of retirement. The messages in society was also the same, do well in school, work hard, go to college, and get a good paying job. The benefit of the American employee, especially the government employee, was that there was security in that job. That job provides safety in a number of ways.

First is the idea of job security. Most workers at the time thought their company would treat them well. It was an expectation that all jobs, especially government jobs, but even corporations, promised a relatively high level of job security. The idea was that a company took care of its own and rewarded loyalty. The majority of workers found the proposition of job security entrancing and remained employees for their entire careers.

Secondly, and more importantly for this book's purposes, was the fact that many jobs also guaranteed retirement for their employees. Employers felt a responsibility to not only protect their workers, but even to make sure their retired workers did not languish in poverty. The most common approach to this was the idea of the defined benefit pension. The employee pays a fraction of their pay into the pension fund. When the fund has vested and they are retired they are promised money from then until the day they die. Not only that, but the employer might also continue offering healthcare coverage to their retirees. The American people relied on these promises. They checked a worry off their life-list. Retirement. Check!

Or was it?

◄ THE RETIREMENT PITFALL

In the past, these promises seemed very attractive. The company will take care of the hospital bills that will almost surely accumulate as you begin to age and the pension is both reliable and secure. People had no need to invest. People would likely say "We're just (insert job here); we don't have the money to invest. We have what we need and trust our job to follow through on its promises. Besides investing is a rich man's game, not to mention dangerous." They were right; their jobs would follow through on its promises. However, they did not see how the world was going to change.

Starting around the 1970s the rate of inflation began to increase in the U.S. dollar and subsequently began to increase in other currencies around the world. Suddenly the rules had changed. The rate of inflation began to devalue those ever stagnant defined benefit plans. The defined benefit pension began to look less and less reliable. For instance, if a pension has no cost of living adjustment and is valued at $60,000, that will forever be the numerical value of the currency offered to that pensioner, but not the actual value. In one year alone that pension will lose $1800 of value in terms of purchasing power assuming an average inflation rate of 3% (which is quite modest these days). Every year the purchasing power, the amount of goods and services that this pension can buy, will decrease.

Employees across America were shocked, the promises they had been given their entire lives suddenly did not seem to be worth anything. "Wasn't retirement taken care of? I remember checking that box quite some time ago." To most retirees their dreams of a comfortable retirement were in shambles. Now they would be forced to live a considerably different retirement. Not the retirement they wanted to live.

Things are not any better now, and there is certainly not any reason to think that things are going to change at all in the near future. According to the U.S. Social Security Administration: From 1980 through 2008, the proportion of private wage and salary workers participating in DB (defined benefit) pension plans fell from 38 percent to 20 percent.[1][2] The trend is moving away from security and to-

INTRODUCTION

ward personal responsibility, such as the defined contribution 401(k) plans, 403(b) plans, or Keogh plans; plans where you fund your own retirement.

It seems the U. S. economy has been moving away from defined benefits for some time now. In fact, the U.S. government has been enacting legislation to encourage it. "Legislation enacted in the 1980s, including the Tax Equity and Fiscal Responsibility Act of 1982 and the Tax Reform Act of 1986, reduced incentives for employers to maintain their DB (defined benefit) plans."[3] Due to laws such as these, companies and government agencies have found it easier to switch their defined benefit plans to defined contribution plans such as the 401(k).[4]

The age of defined benefit has come to an end. So naturally retirees have questions, "So what? Should we be upset about this? Should we write our senators and demand that companies return to a defined benefit system?" If you are upset, sadly your pleas would probably fall on deaf ears. It's likely that both your senator and the people he could influence have both defined benefit and defined contribution plans. To be honest, a reversal is not likely.

In today's current economic climate we cannot resort to the solutions of our parents and the past. In many ways, defined contribution plans do make more sense in today's world. The down sides of defined contribution plans are they may rely almost entirely on your money and are funded by a contribution schedule of your choosing. This may prove dangerous because you then have the choice not to contribute to the plan at all. Defined contribution plans can keep pace with inflation and provide the opportunity for appreciation, but this also means that they can depreciate as the market falls, despite even your best efforts. This may be upsetting to some retirees, but remember, we cannot change what has happened to retirement, it is best that we learn to adapt to it.

As a retiree or someone that will soon be retired you must ask yourself some difficult questions. Did I prepare properly? Do I have a sufficient nest egg? Have I relied on the truths of the past and not

◄ THE RETIREMENT PITFALL

prepared for the new world of retirement? Will I be able to protect what I have accumulated in my estate? Only after honestly answering questions like these and coming to terms with your position can you move forward. Thankfully, there are still ways to correct any mistakes you have made.

The changes that the economy has undergone in the last couple decades and the impact it had on my family has affected the way I see the world and how to prepare for it. Seeing my parents struggle for relying on the broken promises of retirement has taught me one important lesson: It is best to take responsibility for your own retirement. In order to take responsibility you must accept that work, education, and guidance are important tools to get to the retirement you want. If it were easy, everyone would do it. You need to be different, work harder, read more, and get advice.

Many people did attempt these financial responsibilities in recent years. They learned to invest in the stock market and contributed to their 401(k)s. The market flourished in the 1990s and people began to increase the percentage of their savings in stocks. Many then suffered as The Great Recession hit the stock market, costing many seniors and retirees huge chunks of their savings. Again, we cannot change what has happened, we must adapt. The market has changed and people must be more cautious with their money when they are about to retire. Even at retirement age, despite the setbacks you may have encountered on the way here, there are still many things that can be done to ensure that the money you do have lasts for as long as possible.

Moving Forward

We have talked about the past, but to fully comprehend the state that retirement is in today, we must now talk about the present and, more importantly, the future. Specifically, how the economy got to this point and what can be done about it. It may seem like things in the marketplace are beyond your control, but for a successful retirement today one must be prepared to hedge against future market volatility. We will examine the common mistakes that people make when they begin to save for retirement, things that can be done as we approach retirement, and actions that can be taken during retirement to help increase your safety and stability.

Retirement is truly a new phase in life and should be treated as such. This undertaking should be treated like any other phase of your life and you must formulate a good plan to support it. Did you simply walk into a good college one day? Did you just stumble upon your dream job? If you have, consider yourself lucky. Most people work a lifetime to organize these parts of their lives. Retirement should be no different. Having a strong financial plan is the foundation of the "house" of healthy retirement. Inside this house you need multiple pillars to support the roof. Knowledge of Social Security, finding the appropriate investment vehicles for your retirement plan, using insurance to protect assets, understanding the tax system, having proper knowledge of market investments such as stocks and bonds, and planning a solid estate will help create a financial house that is firm against the forces of time, inflation, and government.

This book will address the questions you have regardless of what your situation may be as you approach retirement. Some retirement issues are well known, and others may not seem obvious at first glance. This book will help you recognize and address those less obvious questions to set you apart from the retirement herd.

Some retirees have had difficulty planning properly for retirement, but not being prepared for retirement does not mean that you do not deserve help. A circumstance like an underfunded retirement demands the need for more assistance. It is never too late to work on improving your life. Regardless of your retirement needs, financial planning is the most important factor to enjoying the freedom in retirement you have dreamed of. Financial planning will allow you to live your retirement the way it should be. It can provide something as simple as comfort and stability to luxuries such as grand vacations, all while protecting your valuable estate from unnecessary tax and risk. With a plan, what you get out of retirement can be more than what you put into it.

THE RETIREMENT PITFALL

My sincere hope is this book proves to be a guide in your quest for a retirement that will last and gives you the tools necessary to maximize your experience as a retiree. Now let's answer the question that no one else seems willing to answer, "Retirement planning is great, but what if I'm already retiring?"

INTRODUCTION ENDNOTES:

1. Bureau of Labor Statistics. 2008. National compensation survey: Employee benefits in the United States, March 2008. Bulletin 2715. Washington, DC: Bureau of Labor Statistics.
2. Department of Labor. 2002. Private pension plan bulletin: Abstract of 1998 form 5500 annual reports, Number 11, Winter 2001–2002. Washington, DC: Department of Labor.
3. Rajnes, David. 2002. An evolving pension system: Trends in defined benefit and defined contribution plans. EBRI Issue Brief No. 249. Washington, DC: Employee Benefit Research Institute (September).
4. Munnell, Alicia H., and Annika Sunden. 2004. Coming up short: The challenge of 401(k) plans. Washington, DC: Brookings Institution Press.

CHAPTER 1

Common Fears and Questions

"Courage is resistance to fear, mastery of fear, not absence of fear."
– Mark Twain

FEAR IS ONE of the most basic human emotions. It lies deep within our reptilian brain and springs forth when your brain senses the potential for harm. It is one of the best motivators and also one of the best preventatives known to mankind. Everyone experiences fear. The interesting thing is how people react to it in such dramatically different ways. Some people will flee in outright panic, running at the first sign of danger. Others will freeze in their tracks, gripped by fear in a paralysis of indecision; in terror of their next move. Some will see fear as a challenge and advance resolutely on their problems. In today's world, those who advance on their problems and fears tend to be the most successful. As Mark Twain said, in order to be courageous and overcome fear it must be mastered. In order to master anything you must understand it. In the past, many people thought they had retirement figured out. Most retirees actually looked forward to it as a time of fiscal stability. But today people are increasingly expressing anxiety, stress, and fear about their financial well being. So if people fear what they don't understand, then one might ask, what don't we know now? If the majority of Americans once thought they were well prepared for retirement, what has changed recently? *Why are so many people afraid of retirement?*

Borrow and You Shall Receive

Undoubtedly uncertainty causes fear. Our latest run-in with financial uncertainty and fear is not that far behind us. The Economic downturn beginning in late 2007 and running arguably to 2011 was a financial wake up call, not only for investors, but for most of the American public. Trillions of dollars were lost as the housing market collapsed and people lost everything from their houses to their life savings. The prospect of losing everything that someone has worked for in a lifetime terrified investors and homeowners alike. However, in order to master our fear we must first understand it. What happened? And more importantly, where does that leave us today?

Before the Great Recession and the housing crash of 2007, the U.S. economy seemed unstoppable. The stock market seemed infallible and was habitually reporting double digit annual returns. Investors were euphoric, increasingly abandoning more secure investments for the promise of incredible stock returns. The American public had also forgotten how to live within its means. Americans abandoned their fiscally conservative roots and engaged in some dangerous monetary practices. Credit accounts were so used and abused that some consumers gradually began viewing them as savings accounts. The increasing use of stand-ins for money (such as a credit card or debit card) made it that much easier to pay now and ask questions later. People also began to view luxuries as necessities. Things that had been historically viewed as luxury items like cable, internet, and big-screen televisions began to be seen as must-haves. Consumers began buying bigger and better TVs when their old ones were in perfect functioning order. In fact, sales of the 45in to less than 50in LCD TV segment increased almost 400 percent from 2006 to 2007. [1]

Things that could easily be made were instead bought. People were spending $5 to $10 dollars a day at their local Starbucks where the same amount of spending would land them a pound of coffee at their local super market. Between 1982 and 2007, total spending on food increased by about 16%. As seen in Figure 1.1, "At home" spending has been more or less consistent throughout the years shown. The spending increases shown came almost exclusively from "away from home" food spending, such as restaurants, take out, etc.; items typically seen as luxuries.[2] The graph has also been adjusted to 2008 dollars which means that this is a true increase in household spending on food. American luxury spending was on the rise.

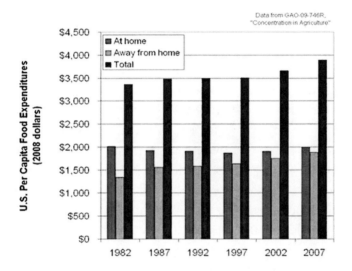

Figure 1.1 Household Spending on Food

I do not write this to say that spending is evil. Spending is fine if one lives within one's means. However, Americans were building a pile of debt. Credit-card debt in the U.S. had reached a record high —nearly $1 trillion, according to figures from the Federal Reserve Board. The average American household's debt from credit cards had risen from $2,966 in 1990 to $9,840 in 2007.[3] According to the Federal Reserve "This nation of the United States has become a "nation of borrowers." If you calculated the 1968 credit debt of $8 billion into 2009 dollars, the current debt would still be over a 2000% increase over the original number."[4] Americans owed $917 billion on revolving credit lines.

$69 billion of it was past due in September 2009.[5] This overspending and over-borrowing was all going to lead to trouble.

A House of Straw

As if the debt and the consumer spending were not enough, there was something even more dangerous happening. Something that people had begun to view as the "safest investment" the average American makes. Something that Americans had been told was a staple of happiness and financial well-being was being abused and misused: Their homes. This aspect of the roaring economy would prove to be the straw that broke the financial camel's back.

Since the beginning of agriculture and civilization, land was something that translated into power. The landed were the elite. They were the lords that would grant their peasants a fief and charge unmentionable amounts of tax for simply allowing the peasants to work the land. In early America, owning land was a prerequisite in order to qualify to vote. During industrialization, the landed gentry lived lives of luxury while the urban poor wallowed in filth. Until this past century, the prospect of owning land was to many a dream, a privilege of the rich, unless you happened to own a farm. Many Americans rented their residences and squandered their hard earned money on rent to the landlord. Americans dreamed of owning their own land. Then as America gained power and influence during the 20th century, it became possible for many to move from cities and own their own homes. After World War II, Americans returned home to a new country. The influx of soldiers soon acquired education, families, and money. This unique set of circumstances led to a housing boom.

Mortgages had also changed. Following the great depression, the government wanted to make it easier for people to obtain a loan. Before government intervention, it was common to only be able to borrow for a home if you already had 50 percent of the value of the home saved. Following the creation of new governmental agencies such as the Federal Housing Administration, the typical down payment was lowered to 20 percent. This payment structure proved to

COMMON FEARS AND QUESTIONS

be stable and reliable. Almost everyone paid their mortgage on time.

America was not the only country that had changed, so had the rest of the world. Following World War II, America was one of the only world economies that had not been absolutely obliterated by the conflict. This meant that the whole world was depending on American products in the post war period. Since America stood alone, they could also charge prices that benefited all Americans. Consequently, a large middle class emerged in America. A middle class that was hard working, educated by the GI Bill, frugal in their spending, and had a strong nesting instinct. This was the perfect storm for the growth of the American suburbs.

The impetus behind the growth of these new homeowners was simple, to own property outright. No longer were Americans throwing their money away to greedy landlords, they were going to own. People that were approved for loans during this time went through tried and true methods for ensuring that they were a safe investment for the bank. They were typically expected to put 20% down on a property with a 30-year fixed rate mortgage. The World War II generation held onto this ethos for most of their lives. Live within your means, own your home. Stable mortgages seemed like the strongest part of the American housing business. Mortgages were so strong that mortgage backed securities were seen as some of the safest investments you could make. After all, home-owners would do anything to keep their mortgage current.

Slowly the idea of homeownership began to change. "Equity" became a word common in the homeowner's vernacular. Literally speaking, equity is the current market value of your home minus the money still owed on your mortgage. To an earlier generation, the issue of equity would likely only come up when selling a house with an unpaid mortgage. To homeowners from the 1980s onward, equity became something synonymous to a personal bank account. If you needed something you could always borrow against the equity in your house. Want a new car? Tap the equity. Vacation? Tap the equity. Home improvement? Tap the equity. You get the idea. Home addi-

◀ **THE RETIREMENT PITFALL**

tions and improvements seemed to be the most popular. After all, you're adding to the value of the home right?

Many people thought this way, borrowing the equity in their house to get themselves out of trouble that they had gotten into in other parts of their life. Many Americans took advantage of their home's value to lighten their credit card debt. Since 2001, more than $350 billion in card debt has been shifted into home-equity loans or into mortgages refinanced by homeowners. [6] The home-equity loans may have less interest than the credit cards, but because of this shifting of debt homeowners began to lose equity in their homes that may have taken years to accumulate.

In the late 1990s and early 2000s this was not a problem. Why? Because home values were appreciating wildly. As long as the value of the homeowner's home kept going up they could continue to borrow against their mortgage and still sell the home at a profit. Then another word crept into the language of the homeowner "refinancing". Why leave all of this new value untapped? Refinance and the bank will give you a new loan based on the newly appraised value of your home. Free money! As long as home values continued to rise...

They didn't.

The whole system came crashing down in 2007 as it became clear that the growth in home prices over the last decade was unsustainable. Right before the bust, The Economist magazine foresaw the trouble ahead claiming "the worldwide rise in house prices are the biggest bubble in history". So if experts saw this crisis coming, why did it happen?

Some believe due to the easing of Credit and Government Regulations such as the Community Reinvestment Act of 1977, [7] banks and lending agencies had begun to give credit to people that otherwise would not have qualified for the loans. The purpose of the CRA was to make sure that all banks that receive Federal Deposit Insurance Corporation (FDIC) insurance be evaluated by Federal banking agencies and make sure that the bank is not discriminatory in its lending practices in any area where they are chartered to do business.[8] In a nutshell, this means that banks had to provide loans to all areas that they were chartered in, even if the area was low or middle income. Supporters of this theory believe that, through the regulation which I am certain was made with the best of intentions; banks were being required to lend to poor credit risks.

Most economists believe and most evidence points to an explanation for the housing crisis that is much more straightforward. The housing market had experienced a large bubble during the 80s and 90s. Banks eventually began to believe that the housing market would never correct itself and began lending more risky mortgages to more under qualified borrowers. As the banks began lend out these sub-prime loans, investors bought them up and began to turn them into mortgage backed securities. All while government agencies sat idle. When the housing market collapsed, everyone involved was in big trouble. Under this theory, the cause of the crisis was overreach by banking institutions, not government overregulation.

Regardless of which theory you believe, all of this easy credit pulled down the standards of loans in general and you began to see all kinds of bizarre mortgage gimmicks. The lender that could offer the more attractive or forgiving loan would get the client, regardless of the loan's stability. Companies were putting themselves out of business. If you did not offer these new products, customers would simply move on to the next guy. Instead of your 20 percent down 30-year mortgages, you begin to see no-money-down loans, some of which would simply ask you to state your income without verifying it. Adjustable rate mortgages would have a low "teaser" interest rate and then the rate would suddenly rise after a year or two. There were interest-only adjustable rate mortgages that allowed people to just pay interest at the beginning of the loan and "payment option" loans where the homeowner pays what they want and any interest not paid is added to the principal of the loan. This type of loan is especially dangerous because the principal is allowed to get bigger. If payment was an issue to begin with it certainly wouldn't get easier if the loan grows! I really cannot think of worse lending practices.

◄ THE RETIREMENT PITFALL

All this debt and horrible lending came to light around 2007 when we began to see the first sub-prime mortgages fail. In turn, this failure began to affect the securities that were backed by these bundled sub-prime mortgages. Mortgage funds fell drastically and pulled the rest of the market with it. Investors that had jumped into the housing market bubble began to pull out of all mortgage backed securities. This resulted in massive losses and the failing of major corporations such as Lehman Brothers, who had gotten too involved in the mortgage securities business. That just got the ball rolling. The rest we saw on the news: the stock market crash, rising unemployment, and of course the two gargantuan bailout packages that America will be paying off for decades to come.

The worst part for most people in the country was the effect that all this had on real estate prices. The home appreciation that everyone had relied on to indulge their every whim had not only flat-lined, but was in an outright nose dive. Of course, many of the people who had received the sub-prime loans went into foreclosure, but the impact of the housing crash was even more profound than that. Homeowners who had taken out loans against their home equity or had recently refinanced suddenly discovered that they are deep underwater on their mortgages as home prices plummeted. Their houses were no longer items that could forgive their credit card debt or give them a new vacation. Now they were stuck trying to pay their mortgage and home equity loans they could not afford or sell the home at a massive loss in a market where the buyer could almost name his price.

Present Day

Many people are afraid. After what has happened, people have a right to be. The events that have unfolded have left many without a plan for retirement. Do you know anyone that was depending on the sale of their home to finance at least a part of their retirement? It was fairly common. Many people lost years of financial gains as they try to recoup not only investment losses but the values of their homes. Many retirees have many urgent questions after what has just hap-

COMMON FEARS AND QUESTIONS

pened to the economy around the world. Will the economy recover? Will the market bounce back? Will I be able to recoup my losses and get back to the retirement I want? Should I do anything different now? Should I give up and hide my money under a mattress?

Obviously hiding your money under a mattress is not the answer, but it is important that we talk about the direction of the economy and if there is anything that can be done. It has been argued that the economy is on the upswing but there are also still many doubts that recovery is possible. Some of these fears stem from the feeling that what has been done so far has been inadequate. Some fear a double dip depression and that the government will not be able to help.

Still, some think the government is the key to stopping the economic crisis. As of writing this book, there is an intense debate occurring in Congress and by the President over whether the economy can be helped through tax hikes or tax cuts. At the center of this heated debate is something that both sides are in agreement about. The U.S. debt is too large. A large part of this debt was created trying to stop the recession from becoming an all-out depression. The Government as of March 2012 has committed $11 Trillion and actually invested $3 Trillion tax dollars in efforts to relieve the beleaguered U.S. economy.[9] Whether this works or not remains to be seen. What is certain is that this is a whole mess of money. Where did it come from?

When I was a child, every now and then the girls on my street would force everyone to play something like house. Though we didn't know it at the time, one part of this game would often be to simulate an economy. The first thing you need to simulate an economy was a currency. We normally would choose something like leaves, sticks, or rocks. Three rocks for this, two sticks for that, and so on. The game would work fine as long as the novelty of the system was respected and the rules were followed, but unfailingly the game would fall apart. Why? We had chosen a currency that was too readily available. There was far too much currency for the goods available and that made the currency devalue. Prices would instantly inflate or business would collapse (we'd quit playing and go home). Frighteningly, with

◄ THE RETIREMENT PITFALL

our currency not attached to any other measure of value, the government can do that same thing. It can endlessly print money.

The government will not just open up the vaults in the Treasury and pull out their rainy day fund to fund programs and projects. The United States has no savings, we're in massive debt. So what does the government do? It prints money: lots of it. The dollar is not actually backed by anything other than the faith and credit of the United States, which is code for you the taxpayer. If the United States does not collect the money to pay its debt it can print money to make up the difference. When the mint prints money it devalues the money that is presently circulating in the economy. Printing money causes the U.S. dollar to inflate. These new programs being used to the stop the recession are costing the U.S. big bucks, but the government has not increased taxes. Ipso facto, this money to pay for these programs is being printed by the U.S. Mint and causing inflation. This means if your dollars are sitting in a vault somewhere or under the mattress after the financial fiascos of 2007 and 2008, you are still actually losing money.

The recession and debt actually make it important to keep your money in an investment vehicle in order to keep up with inflation. Please make sure that you consult with a financial professional before you make any significant changes in the status of your assets.

So we have established that inflation is dangerous, and there is a lot of potential for inflation in the economy right now, but the economy is still in flux. Some believe in the strength of the U.S. economy and its ability to always bounce back. Others believe that this was the beginning of the end; that nothing was fixed and we're all on the precipice of a great disaster. Let us take a quick look at some facts and statistics to understand the state of the economy. Personally, I always like to hear the bad news first and end with the good news fresh in my mind.

COMMON FEARS AND QUESTIONS ❯

The Overall Economy

THE BAD NEWS
- The economy took an enormous hit in 2007 and 2008 and the crisis exposed many of the problems that were plaguing the U.S. economy. The efforts to stop the hemorrhaging of money have cost the U.S. dearly and will continue to cost us for the foreseeable future. The GDP is growing slowly and hasn't reached its pre-recession levels.[11]
- The National Bureau of Economic Research claims that the recession ended in mid-2009. However, unemployment remains high at 8.3% as of Feb 2012[18] and 7.5 percent of the population who are willing to work have given up or taken part-time jobs.[11] Also, the amount of time it is taking the average person to get back to work has increased during the recession from about 13 weeks in the year 2000 to almost 30 weeks in 2010.[13]
- Pensions are drying up. According to Business Insider "Virtually all pension funds in the United States, both private and public, are massively underfunded. With millions of Baby Boomers getting ready to retire, there is simply no way on earth that all of these obligations can be met. Robert Novy-Marx of the University of Chicago and Joshua D. Rauh of Northwestern's Kellogg School of Management recently calculated the collective unfunded pension liability for all 50 U.S. states for Forbes magazine. So what was the total? 3.2 trillion dollars."[13] Medicare and Social Security are facing similar financing issues. Especially with the amount of retiring Baby Boomers just around the corner.[13]
- The rally will likely continue as long as the positive job numbers keep coming in, but investors are still very jumpy. The first sign of weakness in the economy could send the market down again.

◀ THE RETIREMENT PITFALL

THE GOOD NEWS

- Consumer confidence has been rising steadily and more Americans are approving of the direction of the economy. In Early 2012, 30 percent of Americans polled rated the economy as "good" which is the highest level since the question was first asked in 2009. Four out of ten said they expected the economy to get better in the next year and a third of those asked thought unemployment would go down as well, compared to 25 percent that thought the economy would get worse.[10] These may seem like just words, but this is a good sign. Optimism yields real results in things like investing and job creation.
- The unemployment rate is falling. As of the end of February 2012, the unemployment rate had dropped to 8.3 percent down 0.2 percent since December 2012.[12] If March's 2012 numbers come back positive, that means four straight months without a rise in unemployment.

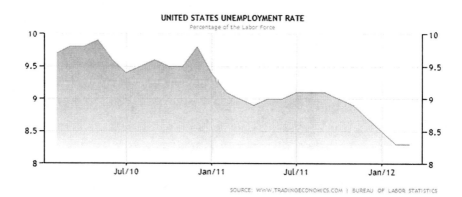

Figure 1.2 - U. S. Unemployment Rate Jan 2010 to Feb 2012.

- Stocks have been on a positive trend as a five month rally continues in March 2012. The S&P 500 has been up eight of the last nine weeks and in early March 2012, it closed above 13,000 for the first time since May 2008.[14]

- Europe's economy is slow due to the recent realizations that countries like Greece are severe credit risks. But it seems as though the European Union may not falter as it loans money to failing parts of its economy. Europe is also borrowing money from the Federal Reserve which could help keep credit moving.[15] Once the EU gets back on its feet that will raise demand for American exports.[15] American exports to Europe could also be aided because the Euro is currently stronger than the dollar.

Is Retirement Obsolete?

There are good things and bad things happening in the economy right now. Uncertainty is high and people are wondering if what they have is enough, even if they were successful in their retirement planning. They know the world has changed.

You are certainly not alone. Most Americans are worried about their retirement. A June 2011 Gallup poll finds retirement is the top financial worry in this country. The poll found that 58% of adults are "very/moderately worried" about maintaining their current lifestyle after they stop working. The number jumps to 77% among 30 to 49-year-olds.[16] In the past, many people invested in real estate for a safer investment, but that norm has been rattled recently. Losses in the value of real estate across the country have wrecked any dreams of doing well on a quick sale of property for the near future. Only those retirees who have owned their homes for at least 10 years should entertain the idea of selling at a profit. Ownership longer than 10 years may be needed to have built up any significant equity.[16]

Pensions are no different. Most pension funds are underfunded or broke to the tune of 3.2 trillion dollars.[13] Things do not look good for the average worker planning on retirement. On top of all this, real incomes are falling. This means, though you may get the same pay year after year, when the boss skips your raise he's actually giving you a pay cut.

Things are simply not as they used to be, but that does not mean

◄ THE RETIREMENT PITFALL

that you should give up. Things may seem less than positive, but now we know what the problem is. Some of these problems are things that must be handled on a national or governmental level, but there is always something that can be done in your life to take advantage of the circumstances as they are. Now you must take responsibility for your own retirement! We all must adapt to the new reality. Complaining accomplishes little; you need action. Please don't leave it up to the government. The recent past has shown how the government manages money.

Get Back in There

The economy is shaky and has not yet proven it is fully out of the recession. It has shown signs that it is on the rebound and making an attempt to come back into an upswing. The full results have yet to be seen, but as an investor it does not make good business sense to wait. Buying high and selling low is the mistake that every inexperienced investor makes. They wait until the market is flush and the prices are high before they buy. Then the market adjusts, the stock drops, and the investor panics and sells at a loss. Don't be an inexperienced investor. The reason that people are afraid to invest in the market right now is because people remember the most recent stock market events. When the stock market was performing great in the 90's, massive returns were expected and attained. More recently, the market has misbehaved, so naturally people believe this to be the new truth about stocks. They believe the market is a dangerous place. However, prices are low and sellers want people back in the market. Proper evaluation of your goals, time horizons, and risk tolerances will determine if it is appropriate for you to participate in the stock market. Now is the time to work with your advisor to determine if it is appropriate for you to be a buyer.

Preparing for Retirement

I know that many of you that read this book may not be twenty-somethings in the position to invest while you are young, but I wouldn't feel like this is a complete book on retirement if I didn't mention the important things to do to while investing at that age. Think of this section as the sage advice that you can hand down to your children or grandchildren when they ask about money.

One thing that often can be done as a young investor is opening a retirement savings account or investment account. Have it taken right out of your paycheck and put into the investment vehicle. You can't miss money that you never see. Also, and this is a big also, it is crucial that you make payments into this account automatic. Don't give yourself the opportunity to cheat and not pay into the account. You should keep a consistent amount of cash flowing into the account in order to increase the principal to help build your retirement assets. If at all possible, participate in your employee sponsored retirement plan. Most employee plans are qualified plans; which means that the contributions are funded with pre-tax dollars. Instead of getting the money and paying taxes on it that year, you will pay taxes on the money when you withdraw from the account. That means that an additional untaxed amount of money has the potential to earn interest or make gains as it sits in your account.

Another thing to remember when you are young is that things change, and they change often. What may have seemed a reasonable expectation or goal last year may suddenly seem too excessive or too easy. Raises, job losses, lawsuits, and windfalls such as market gains and inheritances will all change your financial goals for the future. Be sure to make time once a year to adjust your plan for retirement. Small tweaks can mean a world of difference.

Approaching Retirement – What Can Be Done?

Saving for retirement is daunting in your youth, but normally things calm down, and your personal world slowly changes. You get married, have children, and advance in your career. You also enter your peak earning years in your 40s and 50s and money is easier to come by. The median income for households headed by people in their 50s was just under $64,000 in 2007, according to the Federal Reserve

◄ THE RETIREMENT PITFALL

Survey of Consumer Finances. Median net worth was $229,300, up from $133,100 for people in their 40s.[17]

You pay off the debts of your youth, pay off your mortgage, and the children leave home. Suddenly much more of your money becomes discretionary income. You no longer have to pay down a school loan, a mortgage, or a car payment. This is the point at which many decide to really move forward with their retirement plans. However, as we discussed before, it then becomes a different game to retire comfortable. Beginning young affords you the luxury of having to be being less aggressive in your saving and investing to meet your retirement goals. Now that you are older and in your fifties, the game has changed. What plan can you execute once you have reached age 50?

GET OUT OF DEBT

Debt is the anti-retirement plan. If you are in debt any gain that you make in your investment portfolio could potentially be lost to interest payments on debt. Do not let this happen. Pay off your debt in order to ensure your invested money actually makes you real net gains. The longer those interest payments are around the more you are losing money that could go to your retirement. Try to pay-off your credit cards quickly and do not make the minimum payments. Often the minimum payment will hardly cover the interest accruing on the card. Also, overpay your mortgage and other loans in order to eliminate those sources of debt more quickly.

MAKE YOUR RETIREMENT A PRIORITY

If you still have obligations such as children or debt you need to consider them, but planning for retirement needs to become a major concern for you. If you do not save for yourself and build some sort of savings that you can live on, you will come back to your children as a burden in the long run. That is, if they decide to take you in. Don't put yourself in that position. The kids will be fine without a new car. If they want the finest schools, lend them assistance up to the point that you can afford or see if there are less expensive schools that yield

COMMON FEARS AND QUESTIONS

the same median incomes after graduation. Their higher education is ultimately their responsibility. Make sure to take care of yourself.

Get Your Finances in Order

Finances can get quite jumbled as you save throughout your life. Meet with a financial professional to take a look at your nest egg and see what it will yield in terms of real dollars as you retire. One of the items that likely needs to be investigated is the payout of your pension if you have one. You or your spouse may even have a pension from a previous employer you are unaware of. Knowing about these things could mean the difference between comfort and struggling to make ends meet.

Be aware of developments in the government and your business. It has become popular as of late for companies to make ends meet at the expense of pension plans. One thing businesses and government are trying to do now is change the rules for pensioners by cutting rates and increasing contributions. If this is happening at your job, it may be time to consider leaving to ensure that you will receive the pension that was promised to you. Also, accurately value what your 401(k) or IRA will look like when you retire. Use a conservative appreciation value when trying to determine what your assets will look like when you need them. This way if they over-appreciate that is fantastic, but you are prepared for a more modest scenario.

You may also want to change and/or consolidate all of the investments that you have made over the course of your career. You could take your 401(k) or 403(b) and roll it over into an IRA. If you will have a large income from investments and fall within the income requirements, a Roth IRA could prove to be useful. Roth IRAs contributions are not tax deductible, but the income will not be taxed when you withdraw from the account later on, even on the gains that the account may make. (Please note, in order to qualify for a tax-free, penalty-free withdrawal of earnings in a Roth IRA, the account must have been in place for at least 5 years and the withdrawal must take place after 59 ½.) Using these strategies, you can get your

◄ THE RETIREMENT PITFALL

money ready for the road ahead. Consolidating your funds will also allow you to cut down on the paperwork necessary to maintain your investments and could also cut down on the fees you run into for the management of your investments. IRAs and other various investments will be discussed in greater detail later in this book.

Don't Lose Money to Inflation

The common advice that is given to people as they age is to change their investment portfolio to a more conservative mix of stocks, bonds, and money market funds. While this is good advice, do not take it to the extreme. Transferring too much money from stocks to bonds could allow your money to fall prey to the effects of inflation. You may want to leave a good amount of money in investments designed to beat inflation so that your money will continue to appreciate even when you are retired. Keep in mind that investments seeking higher rates of return generally involve a higher degree of principal risk. However, people are living much longer these days and you do not know how long you may need your funds for. Make sure they last.

Talk About Your Retirement with Your Loved Ones

This may seem silly to say, but you must tell other people what you want in order for them to understand your needs. Far too often I have had clients in that are preparing to retire and in the first five minutes of a meeting it becomes very clear that they have never really discussed retirement with their spouse. You need to discuss and agree on a plan for both retirees if you are a couple. Talk about the age at which you both plan to retire, any individual investments or sources of value you may have, and try to agree on a budget structure for your retirement. Many people believe that they can continue to live their life as if they were still working. Others believe they can increase their standard of living when they retire. Often, this is simply not possible considering the wealth retirees have accumulated. Make sure your plan fits your finances and that all people participating in your retirement are aware of your financial guidelines.

RECONSIDER WHAT IT IS YOU WANT OUT OF RETIREMENT

Do you really want to retire in the way that your parents did? Baby Boomers are notoriously energetic and most retirees now need stimulation in order to stay occupied. Retirement at 65 was more of a necessity in the past. With more people working more physical jobs, it simply was not feasible to work past age 65. Now, work is less strenuous overall and jobs today do not exact the physical toll that jobs of the past did. The possibility of working past age 65 is a real option. If you enjoy your job and you are not quite ready to throw in the towel, work an extra couple years in order to ensure the level of comfort you need for your retirement. Also, think about your expectations in retirement. Will you be taking frequent vacations? What will your spending habits be? Do you plan on having a vacation home? These are all questions that need to be answered.

There is also the option of retiring from your first job and beginning to collect your pension. If you have maxed out your benefits and are at the top of the pay scale an option may be to retire from the first job and take a second to maximize your income. Maybe that second job in addition to your pension will actually make you more money than if you had stayed at your first job. Working as a consultant part-time can be much less stressful and demanding than a full time 9 to 5 situation.

GET A JUMP ON RETIREMENT

As you enter your 50s, many retirement plans also offer catch-up clauses. These clauses allow you to contribute a larger amount of tax free money to your retirement accounts than was previously possible at a younger age. The purpose of these clauses is to allow you, the investor, to "catch-up" on your retirement. Max out any employer contributions to your qualified retirement plan if you are still working. You may have missed the opportunity to have compound interest work for you, but employee contributions to retirement funds are pretty nice as well.

THE RETIREMENT PITFALL

MAKE SURE THAT YOUR ESTATE IS PROPERLY PLANNED

Probate is a messy and time consuming procedure. Properly prepare your estate in order to leave your loved ones what you planned on leaving them immediately instead of years down the road. This book will teach you many procedures that will prevent common mistakes about estate planning, such as double taxation, and the agony of dragging your assets through the government probate system.

STAY AWAY FROM COMMON ADVICE

Common advice yields common results. If common advice worked, everyone would be rich. There is not one fool-proof way to have a successful retirement plan. The unique circumstances that are presented to you in preparation for retirement require a special set of plans. A man with $2 million dollars in assets will definitely need a different retirement plan than someone that has $20,000 in assets. My advice to you is that if a financial advisor or consultant ever pushes a product upon you or provides you with blanket advice without knowing your unique individual circumstances, you should leave immediately. Financial planning is the art of finding what products and services will work best considering the challenges that you, the client, bring to the table.

Some of this advice may seem simple to many retirees, but these steps are the foundation of a successful retirement. Many people that retire feel overwhelmed by the mountain of products and information available to them. It is crucial to remember what your fundamental plan for retirement is as you go through the process of retiring. Do not let the questions or fears you have stop you from making a decision. Action and education are always better than inaction and ignorance when it comes to retirement, even if you realize you were on the right course all along. You must have the courage to take action and master your fear of retirement.

COMMON FEARS AND QUESTIONS

Chapter 1 Endnotes

1. "Big Screen LCD TV sales grow in 2007, research firm says" Broadcast Engineering February 19, 2008.
2. Government Accountability Office GAO-09-746R "Retail Food Prices Grew Faster Than the Prices Farmers Received for Agricultural Commodities, but Economic Research Has Not Established That Concentration Has Affected These Trends" June 30, 2009.
3. "Don't Get Clobbered By Credit Cards!" PARADE.com Web. 2007
4. "Ending the Ignorance: Why the CRA must address Financial Literacy." United States. Federal Reserve July/August 2010
5. "How to Pay Down your Debt" www.consumerreports.org, September 2009
6. USA Today "Home-equity Loans Dry Up" September 2007.
7. "The Global Housing Boom". The Economist. June 16, 2005
8. "Community Reinvestment Act". Federal Reserve Board (FRB). Retrieved Mar 7, 2012
9. Goldman, David. "CNNMoney.com's Bailout Tracker." *CNNMoney*. Cable News Network. Web. 07 Mar. 2012.
10. "Improving Economy Good News For Obama" Associated Press February 22, 2012
11. *"How Can the Economy Recover?" by Jeff Madrick*. The New York Review of Books. Web. 08 Mar. 2012.
12. "Employment Situation Summary." *U.S. Bureau of Labor Statistics*. U.S. Bureau of Labor Statistics, 18 Sept. 2012. Web. 08 Mar. 2012.
13. "20 Reasons Why The U.S. Economy Is Dying And Is Simply Not Going To Recover."*Business Insider*. Web. 08 Mar. 2012. <http://www.businessinsider.com/20-reasons-why-the-us-economy-is-dying-and-is-simply-not-going-to-recover-2010-2>.
14. "Stocks, the Little Engine That Could." *Yahoo! Finance*. Web. 08 Mar. 2012. <http://finance.yahoo.com/news/stocks-little-engine-could-014139722.html>.
15. "U.S. Recovery Can Survive Europe's Recession." *Chicago Tribune*. 15 Jan. 2012. Web. 08 Mar. 2012. <http://articles.chicagotribune.

com/2012-01-15/site/ct-edit-europe-20120115_1_sovereign-debt-global-economy-european-union>.
16. "Retirement As We Know It Is "Dead": EuroPacific's Pento." *Yahoo! Finance*. Web. 08 Mar. 2012. <http://finance.yahoo.com/blogs/daily-ticker/retirement-know-dead-europacific-pento-175638657.html>.
17. "Money in Your 50s: 8 Moves to Make." *MSNMoney*. Web. Aug 2, 2011. <http://money.msn.com/retirement-plan/money-in-your-50s-8-moves-to-make-weston.aspx>.
18. "Employment Situation Summary." *U.S. Bureau of Labor Statistics*. U.S. Bureau of Labor Statistics, 21 Mar. 2013. Web.

CHAPTER **2**

Common Mistakes

"The successful man will profit from his mistakes and try again in a different way."
– Dale Carnegie

Fear…Again

LET US REVISIT fear for a moment, because frankly, it causes many of the mistakes people make regarding retirement. The most common among these mistakes is doing nothing for fear of doing something wrong. I may be beating a dead horse, but I cannot stress enough the negative aspects of inaction and responding reflexively to fearful situations, especially when it comes to preparing for retirement.

Fear is created in a region of the brain known as the amygdale, which processes emotional memories and fear. Some fears all humans are born with; other fears can be learned. The same reason you do not move forward in investing is that same reason you are overcome with terror as you stand on the edge of a large canyon. The basic instinct of fear has kicked in and affected your thinking. You can stand on a step a foot off the floor with no problem. In fact, you could probably dance on it without feeling like you are going to fall. However, when you step up to a larger drop-off you begin to experience vertigo. This is your body's innate attempt to prevent you from doing something incredibly stupid, which in this case would be

◄ THE RETIREMENT PITFALL

plunging to your death. I believe this theory applies to retirement as well. Of course, one fear is intrinsic and the other is learned, but the outcome is the same. Small threats are manageable, larger ones seem impossible. Isn't it easy to save $5 at the convenience store by not buying something you may want? Then why is it that people feel it is so impossible to save responsibly for their retirement?

Of course, the world is very different now than when fear was developed as a human emotion. In prehistoric times, it was essential that a human know whether they were in real physical danger on almost a daily basis. There is still danger in the world, but the chances of running into real physical danger are not the same anymore. Fear does help us not to go down that dark alley, but there are no saber-tooth tigers hunting us. Today, fear can be more of a debilitating emotion than a motivating emotion, especially when confronted with a complex decision. Fear is meant for a fight or flight response, not the intricacies of tax law or estate planning.

Many people are fearful of their finances, and it does not help that many have a very negative view of money. This negativity and fear of money has been taught to us in our culture, and for many of us, in our religion as well. Money is not something that most people talk about and it is certainly a faux pas to ask someone how much they make. Many people would also agree that the quote "Money is the root of all evil" is an accurate assessment. So if so many people have been taught to fear money, how can you make a rational and logical decision involving something that is so emotionally charged? Since money itself is to be feared, then something that involves a large amount of money like retirement would be absolutely terrifying.

However, money is not something to be fearful of, and I will tell you why.

First, everyone that believes that money is the root of all evil has actually gotten their facts wrong. The actual quotation is located in the bible in 1 Timothy 6:10 and it reads: "For the love of money is the root of all evil." This changes the meaning of the verse entirely. The love of money is what causes the problem, not the actual money

COMMON MISTAKES

itself. This I find much more agreeable. Money itself has no power; it is what you do with your money that creates power. Think of money as an extension of your will. If you want something done you have the option of using money to get it done. If you let it sit in a bank your entire life you would have exerted no power with your money. It's a tool. Without an operator it will lay there like an unused hammer. When used properly it can exert a great amount of force. This brings me to something I truly believe to be true about money. If you use your money in wise and generous ways, wealth and generosity will be visited upon you. You use it for greed and evil, it will eventually be your undoing. Money is a means in which you can express your character and values. It does not make you anything, you are who you choose to be.

Another misconception about money is that money can't buy happiness. It is absolutely true that some people are not happy despite the fact that they have millions. However, money will only do what you want it to do. People choose to be happy or sad regardless of the amount of wealth they have. There are people in the best of circumstances financially that are on the verge of suicide; at the same time there are people who are poor who live completely happy lives. This does not mean that it is likely that you would be happy with no money. Money may not directly provide happiness, but it is a factor. If you don't believe me, go and try to live without it for a week.

What money does give you is the opportunity to live a much more comfortable lifestyle. This, in turn, could make people happy by giving them and their loved ones the peace of mind that comes with not worrying how they will pay for things. Money has the ability to provide the comfort that makes happiness more accessible. That's what retirement is about: security for yourself and the continuation of your family legacy. However, many people do not take steps to secure a safe retirement because the perceived threat of making a mistake is so great. Being so fearful makes it very difficult to take action. You are so overcome by the weight of the decision that you do not move, but in reality, moving is what you need to do.

◄ THE RETIREMENT PITFALL

Do You Have a Plan?

Investing and getting ready for retirement can be very different considering the circumstances during investment and the needs of the person wanting to retire. If you want to continue living the life that you presently enjoy without working, obviously that will require more planning and saving than a plan that involves simply having enough to get by.

"What kind of plan should I have?" is a question that people often have on their mind when considering retirement. We will get into what makes the foundation of a generally good plan as the book progresses, but the specifics of the plan typically varies depending on the circumstances of the person in question. By far the most important thing is that you do have a plan. Unfortunately, a large percentage of the U.S. population doesn't have any retirement plan in place. Among the 154.7 million U.S. workers in 2005, 75 million, or 48.5%, did not have a retirement plan or pension offered to them through an employer or union, according to a report by the Employee Benefit Research Institute (EBRI). Small businesses seem to be the biggest offenders of not offering plans to their workers. A Department of Labor 2007 National Compensation Survey found that only 45% of small businesses (those with fewer than 100 employees) offered retirement plans to their employees.[1] For those without retirement plans, it is never too late to start. One simple option may be to have a discussion with your boss about offering retirement plans. The problem may be that he is just not aware of the offerings out there. If you want to go out on your own and try planning outside of work, retirement devices such as IRA, Roth IRAs, and annuities can be a good alternative.

Then there is the issue of timing. If you haven't started investing for retirement the time to begin is now. Studies show that saving early is the easiest way to have enough to enjoy retirement. Living frugally and saving when you are young can pay exponential dividends when you are older. For example, money allowed to compound for forty years can appreciate considerably by the time it is needed. Let's assume that the planned age of retirement is 65. Let's also assume you

COMMON MISTAKES

are 25 years old and invest $2,000 with an average 8 percent return annually. If you do not touch the money and even if you make no additional contributions to the amount, by the time you withdraw that money at age 65 it will still be worth $43,449. If you made that same $2,000 contribution every year at the same rate of return starting at age 25 you would end up with a whopping $561,562. Take the same amount of money and begin an investment with the same rate of return and annual contributions at age 55 and it will be worth $33,291 by age 65.* That is a big difference! In investing, the more time you have the better. The math seems simple right? Everyone should do this. The problem is not many do.

The reason is two-fold: 1. Procrastination 2. Income constraints when you are young.

Procrastination should be a familiar concept to everyone. Procrastination is the act of delaying something that is high priority or stressful for something that is less important or enjoyable. The normal reasons for these delays are that actions that are important usually come with a high degree of stress and therefore are unpleasant to do. The nasty thing about procrastination is that the more you put off the important tasks the more stress and pressure builds up, thus creating more of an incentive to put off those stressful tasks and keep doing things that are enjoyable. So instead of balancing the checkbook or working on that important presentation, you read the newspaper or just wander aimlessly around the house. At one point or another even if you are a highly motivated person, you will put off something that was important to do something less important because it feels better. Unfortunately, many people do feel stress about retirement and therefore would rather think about it tomorrow. They would rather not make those hard decisions today that would result in a better life down the road. To some, making these tough retirement decisions may affect

---

*Hypothetical example used for illustrative purposes. Actual results may vary. Investments seeking higher rates of return generally involve a higher degree of risk of principal. Example does not take in account the consequences of fees or taxes and is not indicative of any specific investment.

THE RETIREMENT PITFALL

luxury spending like shopping or eating out. To others these decisions can affect their standard of living which can make saving extremely difficult. In either scenario, most people prefer to think about retirement tomorrow; even when retirement may be tomorrow.

Many people also do not create a financial plan for their retirement because they are hesitant to meet with a financial advisor. This is normally because they think it is not necessary, the sum they have accumulated is not acceptable, or they feel that action will result in an irrevocable mistake. In fact, most Americans don't meet with a financial advisor and the Americans that do see an advisor are typically the wealthy. Employees in households with $125,000 to $199,999 in yearly income are significantly more likely to use a financial adviser (44 percent) than households earning $74,999 or less annually (between 16 and 18 percent). And only about a quarter (27 percent) of those earning between $75,000 and $124,999 get professional financial planning advice.[2] This means that people who may be in need of financial advice are not getting the help they need. In fact, only 36 percent of Americans actually have a financial plan according to a 2009 National Consumer Survey on Personal Finance conducted by the Certified Financial Planner Board of Standards; the survey collected data from 1,700+ U.S. residents. Additionally, only 17 percent of those polled have a written financial plan that is updated regularly and reviewed in light of changing times.[3]

It is clear that many people do not plan the time that is necessary to have success in their personal finances. It is imperative that no matter what stage you are in life, you need to start taking action. No effort is too late to create a plan or to take action for your retirement.

You should not feel bad if you did not begin saving a large amount at age 25, few people are fortunate enough to have a large savings later on in life, let alone at such a young age. Do you remember when you were a very young child, maybe say 10 years old? Remember the value you placed on $1,000 dollars? The reason that you viewed that money differently was not because it was more valuable (which is technically true taking into account inflation), you valued it dif-

COMMON MISTAKES

ferently because of the way you viewed its uses. To a ten year old the $1,000 dollars would be purely discretionary spending. Games, toys, candy, you name it it's yours. The amount of things you can get with that $1,000 seemed endless and you had little responsibility; consequently you did not appreciate the true value of the money. You mainly viewed money as a way to get things you wanted; what you needed came free from your parents.

As you get older you begin to view money differently. The things that you took for granted as a child suddenly cost money. Now that $1000 dollars takes on a whole new meaning. You need $800 for rent, $100 for energy, $100 for cable... before you know it *poof* the money is gone and you have no money to enjoy. When you are in your 20s, typically the entry level job you take does not offer a salary that is much more than the amount you need to get by. Any discretionary spending that you have is highly valued and it is very difficult to part with. As you become more successful in your 40s and 50s, it becomes hard to remember what that money meant to you in your youth. At the time that money had a high intrinsic value to you and parting with it for a retirement fund was extremely difficult, if it even crossed your mind at all. The limited discretionary income that you did have needed to be spent on things that made you happy; there was enough pressure just to make ends meet. Your mind was very far from ideas of what your plan for retirement would be like.

In addition to the intangible feelings many people have about money when they are young, there is also some hard facts to prevent retirement planning and saving in your 20s and 30s. When people come out of college they have normally accumulated a large amount of debt. They are then thrust into the working world where many new demands are put on them. You need a car, you need clothing, you need an apartment, and the list goes on. All of this translates into debt. Few people have the money to afford these things and must borrow. If you are investing while letting interest accumulate you are spinning your wheels. If you have a $10,000 loan that charges 8% interest annually and you have a $10,000 investment fund that yields an 8% return, you have broken even. Nothing is being accomplished. People in their twenties are more than twice as likely as older folks to have a negative net worth; one out of four families headed by people aged 20 to 29 owed more than they owned.[4] Investing while simultaneously losing money in debt interest is a fool's errand. When you are young it is first important to get yourself out of debt. Something that many people assume of young investors is that they start without debt, which is definitely a flawed assumption.

Despite the things that may have caused you to not plan in the past, you should begin to plan now. It is never too late to start and many advisors will assist you regardless of how much you have saved. Better late than never!

Do You Have Proper Advice?

In order to make money and retirement work for you, you must not make the mistake of treating money like it is dirty. Talk to people about money; learn how others who retired successfully did it. Don't give in to the fear mongering of people claiming to have been ripped off by financial professionals. Are there bad financial advisors out there? Yes. Are there bad doctors? Yes. Are there bad dentists? Yes. Can you not see a dentist or doctor because there are bad ones out there? No! You need their services. Do your research and find out who you can trust. Talk to financial professionals openly and honestly about the condition of your finances like you would talk to your doctor about the condition of your health. Then, like a doctor, a financial advisor can properly diagnose any problems and offer treatments to help you achieve financial well being.

How To Find a Good Advisor

Good financial advisors are people that truly do care about their clients and take their client's financial needs, wants, and concerns very seriously. They know that your finances and your retirement are some of the most important aspects of your life and treat these topics with the respect that they deserve. However, there also is the possibility that you may find an advisor that does not have your best interests at heart, but you can avoid them if you know what to look for. Use the following benchmarks to discern the good advisors from the bad advisors.

EVALUATE YOUR INVESTMENTS:
- Know how the investments under his control are performing. That does not mean if you lose some money that the financial advisor is no good. When the market goes down, almost everyone loses money. Those that make money in a down market are very rare. The point of a retirement investment is long-term appreciation; do not get upset if you experience some temporary setbacks.
- A good way to evaluate your investments is to compare the performance of the products that your advisor recommended against the appropriate benchmarks. If the benchmark drops 5% you should not be concerned if your investments drop 3%. If the benchmark drops 5% and you lose 7% value on your investments, then it is time to be concerned. This type of loss could indicate that there is something wrong with your investments, or that they are too risky. Some advisors will want to make a high risk portfolio in order to achieve high returns. This may not be a wise investment strategy for you. Make sure that your advisor is aware of your willingness to engage in risk and your needs as an investor.

THINGS TO WATCH OUT FOR:
- If your advisor immediately presents you with a product without properly getting to know you, that could also be a red flag. Each person that seeks out a financial advisor has a different financial situation. Also, people in similar financial situations may have drastically different wants and needs. Someone may expect to live in the lap of luxury in retirement while others are happy living modestly. Without knowing their client, it is

THE RETIREMENT PITFALL

almost impossible for a financial advisor to give assistance in a meaningful way. There are many financial products out there and each is made to meet a certain need. Your advisor should be your financial tailor; fitting the product to what you want out of retirement. Be wary of the advisor that does not ask questions before pitching you a product. It may be a cheap suit or a suit that fits that advisor better than it fits you.

- An advisor should also adhere to basic standards about what an investment portfolio for someone at a given age and with a given income should look like. If you are 55 years old and your advisor has 90% of your assets in stocks that is not by any means standard. The general rule of thumb is as you get older; your investments should become more conservative. You may discuss your desire to make your portfolio more risky, but that advice should not come from an advisor unless your aims demand a more aggressive portfolio.
- Another thing to be wary about is if an advisor tries to push a product based on past performance. This is an attractive pull for many people that are not well versed in the financial services industry. However past performance is not an indicator of future performance. Always have your advisor give logical reasons why you should have a specific investment product. Does it aid in your aims for retirement? Does the manager of the fund have a record of beating the market? Are there political or regulatory happenings that will help this industry? Does a specific stock have a good price to earnings ratio? These are measurable indicators that could potentially lead to the price of a stock rising. The fact that a stock has risen in the past or the fact that a stock price is high in no way means that it will continue to rise. Often it actually means it is too late to make any real gains in the stock. Do not make the mistake of falling for the past performance approach. Make sure your advisor is not selling you his product, but is selling you your product; the product that you need.

COMMON MISTAKES

TRAITS OF A GOOD ADVISOR:

- A good advisor most importantly will get to know you as a person. This may seem to be just a friendly gesture, but as a financial planner it is important to know the wants and needs of the client. After all, money is the conduit in which you obtain many wants and needs. An advisor that asks questions and listens is an advisor that will be able to suggest financial strategies that work for you; not just what fund is hot at the moment. Your advisors knowledge of you will help him better understand your financial goals. That way investment decisions could always be made with your goals and values in mind.
- A good investor will also try to reduce risk as much as possible while still maintaining your investment objectives. There are many investment tools out there and all of them vary in the amount of risk that they carry. They also vary in the amount of returns that they generally yield and the ways in which those returns are given to the client. Of course, an advisor wants to help your portfolio appreciate, but what is most important is what you actually want from life. A good advisor should minimize the amount of risk necessary to help you retire in comfort, not increase risk in hopes of a huge return only to see your life savings slip way. Your money is not a game; it is a means to reaching your goals in retirement.

Are You Making Excuses?

My father was not one to strongly express his opinions, but he did stress to me his thoughts on excuses in the best way that he knew how. "Excuses are like armpits, everyone's got them and they all stink." There are more colorful variations of this euphemism that I have come across, but they all boil down to essentially the same thing. Whenever some people do something wrong, they always come up with an excuse. Except for in some very seldom circumstances, excuses are commonly just a way of deflecting blame or hiding a lack

◄ THE RETIREMENT PITFALL

of commitment or responsibility. Excuses can also assist people in incorrectly rationalizing why they should not be doing something; like saving for retirement.

Instead of attempting to achieve something, they will convince themselves that the results will not be acceptable considering the amount of time necessary to complete the task. Commonly, excuses are one of the only things that stand between average people and being successful. Why then do people make excuses? It is a strategy that many people have developed because they fear failure. However, people often allow themselves to fail by making excuses. Therefore, we must understand why people fail in order to overcome the fear of failure, stop making excuses, take action, and reach success.

There are common reasons people fail:

- <u>Failing because we do not believe in what we are doing from the very beginning</u>. We beat ourselves before we are beaten. Why would you attempt something if you believe in your mind that you will fail? You are setting yourself up for disaster. You must convince yourself that what you want is possible, you are the one that can do it, and you will take action now. Remember, whether you think you can, or you think you can't, you're right.
- <u>Failing because when presented with the situation they shut down</u>. If you have brought yourself to the point where you have to perform the task, why not give an attempt that has the possibility of success? Anything worth having takes work.
- <u>Failing because they are not true to themselves</u>. Be honest about what you want from life. If you compromise on your desires you are just setting yourself up for something that does not make you happy. How does that make any sense?
- <u>Failing because they feel sorry for themselves</u>. Some retirees will become hopeless about their prospects of having a happy retirement and wallow in their own self-pity. Do not allow yourself to be a victim. Keep yourself away from people that bring negativity into your life. Take action and make progress

COMMON MISTAKES

toward your goal. Nothing ever got done by sitting still.
- <u>Failing because they quit</u>. Quitting in the middle of something makes all the previous work absolutely useless. Why start if you are going to convince yourself half-way through that you shouldn't have started in the first place. Follow Through!
- <u>Failing for self-validation</u>. This may be the worst of all reasons people fail. They have imagined that something about themselves or the world is unfailingly true. They may believe something like "they are too fat" or that "people do not like them" but instead of trying to prove people wrong, they engage in behavior that validates their belief and then use their belief as an excuse. You will never get anywhere with that thinking.

Take these reasons for failure and really think about them. At one time or another negative thoughts will cross your mind, but you must train yourself to work towards your goal and not let yourself fail. You can be your own worst enemy or you can be an invaluable ally. The choice is yours.

With failure often come the inevitable excuses. There are a number of excuses that resonate throughout the financial planning industry concerning retirement. Most of them are based primarily on the fear of not building an acceptable retirement. We must overcome that fear and stop making excuses. I will now refute common excuses that hurt retirees in their quest for retirement planning in order to show you that no excuse is good enough to cheat yourself out of success. Be honest with yourself and see if you have ever thought or used any of these excuses as a reason to not start a plan for retirement:

- <u>I Don't Need To</u> – Some people believe that they have saved so much money that they do not need a retirement plan. This could not be further from the truth. Often people with large savings have the inclination to overspend. The number looks big, so you begin to really dig into it at the beginning of your retirement. Flying around the world, buying country club memberships, doing all the things you always wanted to do

◄ **THE RETIREMENT PITFALL**

with your money. The problem is that your number normally needs to last at least 20 years. If you spend all your money jet setting around the world, it may be difficult to enjoy the final years of your retirement. Those years often much more expensive than most people think. Not because you are enjoying yourself, but because medical expenses can quickly get out of control. It is crucial to always have a plan. Failing to plan is planning to fail.

- It's Too Soon – It is never too soon to invest for retirement. The sooner you start saving for retirement the better. Remember the power of compounding on your money.
- I'm Too Busy – This is just a way that people procrastinate. Everyone is busy. What separates the people that are unsuccessful and the people that are successful is the extra effort. Everyone goes to work every day, but not everyone takes the time to go the extra mile and make sure their futures are in order. Take responsibility for your retirement!
- I Don't Have the Money – The objective of investing is to get you the money that you will need in order to enjoy your retirement. Saying you don't have enough money but not investing is like saying you are hungry but not eating. If you have any discretionary income at all, especially in your later years, this money should go toward your retirement. Putting anything toward your retirement is better than nothing.
- I Have a 401(k) – A 401(k) is a great way to save for retirement, but it is not a retirement plan. Once you are ready to begin retirement, the 401(k) is a just lump of money waiting for you to take distributions out of it. You need to have a plan to use the 401(k) in order to make it last.
- I'm Happy With What I Have - Maybe you do have a retirement plan. That's great! But always remember that the world is changing and you are changing. As you age more and more, you want to have more secure investments that you can rely on to provide income. Always update your plan and update

COMMON MISTAKES

your finances. As Francis Bacon said "He that will not apply new remedies must expect new evils; for time is the greatest innovator."

- <u>I Have Too Many Other Obligations</u> – It is important to pay down your own debt, but you need to be a little selfish when it comes to always helping others. For instance, you may want to help your children afford college, but in the last analysis it is their debt, not your debt. They can borrow for their education; you can't borrow for your retirement. Besides if you save poorly for retirement the responsibility to take care of you may fall to them. If you really want to help them out, help yourself first.
- <u>I Don't Know How</u> – If you don't know how to invest or find the prospect of investing intimidating you should seek out advice, not hide from it. If you don't like how things turn out you can always change your investments. There are advisors out there that have your best interests at heart. Seek them out and get their advice.
- <u>It's Too Late</u> – I spent most of the end of Chapter 1 explaining things you can do later on in your life in order to prepare for retirement. Getting out of debt, using catch up clauses on retirement portfolios, organizing your estate, and communicating what you want out of retirement are all things that can be done as you approach retirement. If you are already of retirement age it is still not too late. Reorganizing your payments and the way that you receive your retirement income can have a tremendous impact on its staying power.
- <u>The Government Will Take Care of Me</u> – The government is in some serious trouble because it spends far more than it collects. Do you believe that this type of spending is sustainable? There will almost surely be change in the way the government spends and collects money in the near future. When you say that you are counting on the government to take care of you, you are counting on the government fixing its financial

◄ THE RETIREMENT PITFALL

crisis while not cutting two enormous drains on the budget: Medicare and Social Security. That is a bet I would not take. I believe change is coming.

Don't let yourself fall victim to these excuses. For every excuse you come up with not to invest, there is an equally good reason to work on your retirement plans. Doing something is moving in a positive direction. You can always make changes if you are not happy with the results.

Your Home is Not an Asset

Homes are one of the most misunderstood parts of many people's lives. Many people believe that by virtue of having a home, they are then richer because they are building equity. This is a poor way to view your home because your home is not building you anything.

I am not saying that owning a home does not have advantages. In the recent past, the values of homes in the United States were moving up with no end in sight. If you paid $33,000 for a house in 1967 and sold it in 2006 for $550,000, the annual return would be about 7.5%. If you missed the peak and sold this year for $375,000, you'd still have about a 6% annual return. Adjusting for inflation, $33,000 in 1967 would be equivalent to about $213,000 today, meaning you would still be making money with the sale of your home even in inflation adjusted dollars.[5] Appreciation is nice, but that is not the only reason to own a home. There is tax incentives associated with owning a house, houses may be used as collateral on loans, you may refinance the home for money, and you also may borrow against the equity you have in the home.

However, we must understand the actual relationship we have with our homes. When we take out a mortgage we are asking the bank to pay the seller for us. The bank lends us the money to pay the seller and in return we have to pay a mortgage. A mortgage is a debt, when you pay a mortgage and build equity you are simply paying a debt that you can borrow back if need be.

Homeowners in the past treated their homes like they should be treated, as a place to live. They took time to save the 20% needed to buy the home and they made their payments every month until they had paid off their mortgages. Their homes appreciated in value, but it was value that they did not count on until their house was sold. They did not borrow money using equity as collateral. They cared for their home because it was where they lived, it was a source of pride, and they expected their neighbors to do the same. They also knew everyone caring for their homes helped maintain the general value of homes in the community. They knew that their house was a liability and worked hard to make sure that their home was not adding to their overall debt. Homeowners in the past knew something that it seems most people have forgotten now.

Your home is not an asset. An asset is something that creates money. For all homeowners that have a mortgage your home is a liability, it is drawing money out of your bank account. Even if your home is paid off it is still a liability. The insurance, property taxes, and upkeep you pay on your home every year pulls money out of your pocket. On top of all this, mortgages that have been lent in the years before the 2007 recession were especially dangerous because they were often ways to give people a home they could not afford. They were certainly not safe investments.

Thankfully, mortgages have changed in the last 5 years. Increasingly rare are the easy no-money-down loans and the tricky mortgages that caused the financial meltdown we are paying for today. Now, the most forgiving mortgages normally begin with the 3.5% down required for an FHA loan. Some lenders have abandoned the newer loan structures completely and have reverted to the standard 20% down 30-year mortgage plans. Gone are the days of the easy loans; old is the new trend as lenders are asking borrowers to show stable employment, good credit, and a large down-payment.

The equity in your home is money that you have already paid to the bank, less interest. Do not be fooled into thinking that the home you live in makes you wealthy. Equity can be a valuable tool when used responsibly, but it is really just a payment on a debt; if used it must be used with care. If there is an emergency it can mean the difference between losing control of your finances and keeping your head above water. It is a place to go for your absolute needs not your trivial wants.

If your home appreciates in value you still have not turned your home into an asset. The increase in value is an unrealized gain. If you do not sell the house that number might as well mean nothing to you. That is why refinancing your home is dangerous. A bank may give you a new loan amount because the appraised value of your home went up. The problem is you do not have that appraised value unless you sell the house. If the price of the home drops the day after you refinance, you are suddenly underwater on your home because the refinanced value is greater than the new appraised value of your house. Always remember the appraised value of your house is not a promise of a future realized gain. Many people found that out the hard way in the last couple years.

This does not mean that real estate cannot be an asset; it just means the house you are living in cannot be an asset. The home you live in is a liability because it takes money out of your overall assets.

What Should I Do?

- Pay down your mortgage. If possible try and pay back the mortgage on the home you live in as quickly as possible. For many people their home payment is the largest cost that they have on a monthly basis. Imagine what you could save and invest if you freed that money up every month. Paying off your home will pay huge dividends in retirement. Be careful though, some mortgages have penalties for paying off early.
- See if refinancing will benefit you. If you are in trouble with your home a way to avoid foreclosure or bankruptcy is by refinancing. By refinancing you make it possible to have a lower monthly payment by getting a better interest rate, lowering your monthly payments outright, or changing the interest rate from adjustable-rate to fixed-rate. You can also

obtain cash from refinancing, but you should be very careful how you spend this money. Many people were careless with refinanced home loans and were ruined as housing prices dropped. If you are planning on refinancing make sure your credit is good because credit is what they will base most of their refinanced terms on. Before you make any refinancing decisions, please consult a legal or financial professional to determine if that is the right move for you.

- <u>Make sure you know how much your house will contribute to your retirement</u>. Retirees should not make the mistake of factoring in the full value of their home as retirement savings, especially if you are still paying a mortgage. For instance, if the value of your home is $500,000 dollars and you have a $200,000 outstanding either from a mortgage or from borrowing against your home, you can only rely on $300,000 for your retirement. That is if you manage to sell the house at full value. Also, where is that money going after you sell your house? Are you moving in with family? Will they expect contributions from you for their expenses? Are you buying a new place? Many retirees do downsize, but even a downsize costs money. Of the $300,000 previously mentioned maybe a comfortable condo costs somewhere in the ballpark of $200,000. The house that you thought was going to finance your retirement really only netted you $100,000 in retirement income. How long will that last you in retirement? Don't rely on your house to fund your retirement. Your house is not an asset.

Dealing With Family

People feel many different ways about their families and nearly every family is different. There is only one rule that applies to everyone, we are stuck with our families for better or for worse. Families can be a source of inspiration and strength and they can also be an enormous drain on your resources, physically, emotionally and financially. Typically the most difficult thing about family is when they

◄ **THE RETIREMENT PITFALL**

come to you it is your responsibility to help them. Refusal is not an option.

When things are difficult, family are the people that you go to. They are the ones that will always be there when you need them, but when you are the one that is needed, that can put unforeseen stress on you and your finances.

Finances in families are vastly different than they used to be. Take kids for instance. How many toys did the average kid have as you were growing up? In true form to their frugal existence, the parents of Baby Boomers did not spend exorbitant amounts on their children. I personally had a few toys here and there; the most valued of my possessions being my bike. Today there is no end to amount of things children are expected to have. They need toys when they are young to promote their learning, they need more toys to keep them active, and then toys like video games to keep them occupied. Even in adulthood, it seems that this trend is continuing. The online poll by Forbes Woman and The National Endowment for Financial Education (NEFE) of 1,074 U.S. adults—non-students aged 18 to 39 and their parents found that 59% of parents provide financial support to their adult children who are no longer in school.[6] Boomers, don't think the children are to blame either. Supporting and enabling are different things. When you indulge your children's every whim and paid their way through school, your actions have led to less money going to your retirement.

Also, in this tough economy it is also not uncommon to see children staying with their parents longer. A study by the U.S. Census Bureau shows that 59% of men ages 18 to 24 currently live with their parents, an increase from 53% in 2005. Likewise, 50% of 18-to-24-year old women currently live at home, an increase from 46%. In the 25-to-34-year old age bracket—males living at home increased to 19% from 14%,. Similarly, the number of young women returning to the nest rose to 10% from 8% in the last six years.[7]

This is not a historical anomaly. In fact, until the baby boomer generation it was common for adult children to stay in the house at least until they were married, or maybe even longer. The difference with adult children living at home these days is they are not contributing to the finances of the household as much. In fact, a study by a professor of human development and family sciences at Oregon State University found that parents are spending 10 percent of their annual income helping their adult children.[8]

Families are also living longer. The likelihood that elderly parents may move into their middle-aged children's homes for financial or health reasons is increasing. Many people are now outliving their investments and are forced to fall back on family, creating a further strain on people that then have to support them. Since 1990, the number of multigenerational households has grown about 40 percent. That's 50 million Americans or 16% of the population that has more than a nuclear family.[9] With the parents of Baby Boomers moving into their 70s and 80s, this number with surely increase.

Having your parents in your home presents a number of new challenges to your everyday routine. The adaptation to your changing family roles may be difficult to navigate. Additionally, there are the annoyances of less room and less privacy. All of this adds up to less of an opportunity to make money and more of an obligation to spend money. Be sure that you don't stretch yourself too thin caring for others. Eventually your financial malfeasance will fall on the shoulders of your children if you are not careful.

One mistake that some people make as they begin to care for their aging kin is that they maintain the same family structure as there was in the past. If you are the head of the household and providing for the family it is important that you take control of the house. Your parents need to know that it is your house and that things have changed. This should not be because of some anger or resentment toward your parents, but for their benefit. It is important to tell your parents that you need to be aware of their finances. With this knowledge, you could have them help with the additional expenses around the house with their pension or share some of their social security as a type of rent. More importantly, this information could protect them. The elderly are unfortunately common victims of fraud and financial scheming.

THE RETIREMENT PITFALL

Having knowledge of your parent's finances could keep them from making a mistake that could harm the whole family.

The new financial realities of today have many families in a tough position. Ultimately, how much you devote to your family is a lifestyle decision. It can be incredibly difficult to say no to a loved one, but sometimes you have to be cruel to be kind. By lifting their burden now you will just make yourself the burden later. You don't have to abandon your loved ones, just make sure that they know there is a limit on what you can provide them. Make your retirement a priority.

Other Common Mistakes

There are a myriad of other mistakes that people will make that can harm their nest egg. One thing that people commonly do is pull money out of their 401(k) while they are still working and under 59 ½. This is definitely something I would avoid at all costs. Pulling money out of your 401(k) can have significant effects on your retirement. A further discussion of how to avoid the pitfalls of dipping into your 401(k) will be discussed in the retirement plans chapter of this book. This chapter will show you how to maintain a healthy 401(k) and how to transfer 401(k)s to retirement accounts.

Not diversifying your portfolio is another pitfall that many people succumb to. Most people know that diversifying your portfolio is a way to hedge against risk in your investments, but most do not know that many people think they are diversifying when they really are not.

Hopefully this chapter has pointed out any faux pas you are making in your retirement savings, and has given you strategies to fix these problems. Mistakes are unfortunate, but they are a part of life, especially when dealing with something as complicated as retirement planning. Do not let setbacks keep you from trying to succeed. Take your failures and learn from them. Thomas Edison tested hundreds of materials in his laboratory before he invented the light bulb that we know today, and he is considered a genius not a failure. As you read on remember, the weak let their mistakes dominate their lives. The strong will learn from their mistakes and try again until they reach success.

CHAPTER 2 ENDNOTES

1. "SmartMoney." *Alternatives for Those Without Retirement Plans.* Web. 15 Mar. 2012. <http://www.smartmoney.com/retirement/planning/alternatives-for-those-without-retirement-plans-21933/>.
2. "How Much Money Do You Need to See a Financial Adviser?" - *Planning to Retire (usnews.com).* Web. 09 Mar. 2012. <http://money.usnews.com/money/blogs/planning-to-retire/2011/06/21/how-much-money-do-you-need-to-see-a-financial-adviser>.
3. Hudson Valley Business Journal, 11/9/2009, Vol. 19 Issue 44
4. "Your 20s: Planning Pays off Richly." *MSNMoney.* Web. 09 October 24, 2011. <http://money.msn.com/retirement-plan/your-20s-planning-pays-off-richly-weston.aspx>.
5. "Don't Bank on Your Home as an ATM." *Los Angeles Times.* Los Angeles Times, 27 Sept. 2009. Web. 15 Mar. 2012. http://articles.latimes.com/2009/sep/27/business/fi-cover-housing27
6. Goudreau, Jenna. "Nearly 60% Of Parents Provide Financial Support To Adult Children."*Forbes.* Forbes Magazine, 20 May 2011. Web. 19 Mar. 2012. <http://www.forbes.com/sites/jennagoudreau/2011/05/20/parents-provide-financial-support-money-adult-children/>.
7. "Boomerang Kids: How Long Should They Stay?" *Fox Business.* Web. 19 Mar. 2012. <http://www.foxbusiness.com/personal-finance/2011/11/04/boomerang-kids-how-long-should-stay/>.
8. "Study: Young Adults Linger at Home Longer." *Gazettetimes.com.* Web. 19 Mar. 2012. <http://www.gazettetimes.com/news/local/article_a0a7b8cc-5272-11df-bbdf-001cc4c002e0.html>.
9. "More Elderly Parents Moving in with Children." *More Elderly Parents Moving in with Children.* Web. 20 Mar. 2012. <http://www.dallasnews.com/business/personal-finance/headlines/20110610-more-elderly-parents-moving-in-with-children.ece>.

CHAPTER 3

Spending/Old Habits

"You cannot keep out of trouble by spending more than you earn."
– Abraham Lincoln

SPENDING HAS BECOME something of a national pastime in America. People habitually spend more than they can afford. We spend so much, some have begun to refer to spending as an addiction or disease (e.g. shopaholic). Curiously, it is also often referenced as a cure to what ails you (e.g. retail therapy). People certainly have very different feelings on money, its use, and its overuse. As we have discussed, people in the United States typically outspend their earnings and end up in a large amount of consumer debt. If you are spending more than you earn you certainly won't have an opportunity to save for retirement. This is a fate that befalls far too many Americans every year. This chapter will be dedicated to understanding why you spend money and what can be done about breaking bad financial habits.

Until recently, money around the world was normally backed by a valuable commodity such as gold. Everyone around the world could agree that gold is valuable so nations would use gold to back their currencies. Under this system, if you wanted to increase the money supply without devaluing the currency the amount of gold that the country possessed needed to go up. This system was typically stable because if the country had enough gold to back their currency, inflation and deflation was unlikely. However, this theory of money also does not allow for rapid adjustments to conditions in an economy, because in order to increase the money supply, you have to secure more gold. Because of this economic shortfall, most economies abandoned the gold standard in the 20th century. Most countries today accept that the modern value of money is determined by the forces of supply and demand. If the money is in high demand and in low supply the value of the money goes up. If there is high supply and low demand, the value will go down. This system is called a fiat money system, and it is the system that the United States and many other countries around the world adhere to today.

One symptom of a fiat money system is inflation, and inflation could encourage spending. As we know, inflation is the devaluing of a currency, meaning it takes more money to buy the same products every year. Since money is devaluing every year it is no longer advantageous to simply hold money, but you may invest it to try to increase your wealth and keep pace with the rate of inflation. If you do not invest money, then inflation often encourages you to spend money to avoid it devaluing while in your possession, thereby destroying your purchasing power. However, besides homes or maybe cars, most consumers don't buy in ways that protects their purchasing power, such as buying for appreciation or resale value, they buy things to use. Most consumers do not spend to preserve the value of their dollar. Yet we continue to spend instead of invest.

Perhaps the government is to blame. The U.S. government has been known to give incentives to spenders. When the airline industry went bad in 2001, George W. Bush told Americans to take a trip to Florida. When the housing market crashed, there was an $8,000 tax credit for anyone who bought a home in 2008 and 2009. Some of these tactics and policies work, and some do not, but the government does attempt to induce spending.

Forces in our economy do encourage spending, and all of them are viable explanations for why Americans spend, but these same forces could encourage investing as well. For instance, the govern-

◄ **THE RETIREMENT PITFALL**

ment changes interest rates in order to encourage investment and also gives many investments far more favorable tax rates than things such as ordinary earned income. So then why do we spend more than we invest? I could go on all day about how the government may or may not want us to spend, but it is really much more simple than all this. The truth is we spend because we want to. America has been a wealthy country for such an incredible stretch of time there are not many people alive today that remember when it wasn't. Spending is a national past-time and we do it because we like it. It makes us feel good.

Money Is Emotional

Money is not what you want; money is the way to get what you want. People spend for emotional reasons. If you ask someone what they would do if they suddenly came into a large amount of money, rarely do they tell you the first thing they want to do is increase their investment portfolio. If they do say that, you won't have to probe much further to find the emotions and wants behind that decision. People want to satisfy that "now" need. They want the new house, the new car, the new boat, and the grand vacation. For the most part, people are emotional with spending.

When you retire, it seems that most people think that this is the time they will use their money to realize their dreams. Maybe their dream is to go back to school and learn another language, maybe your dream is to travel the world, or maybe your dream is to get closer to the ones you love. Regardless, all of these wishes are for deep emotional wants such as freedom, enrichment, or companionship. If you are constantly spending emotionally when you are young, the chances of you being able to enjoy those retirement dreams gets farther and farther away.

Unfortunately for most of us, the world is often working against us. Modern psychology has significantly improved its understanding of how people view and spend money. This is unfortunate because most of the time this knowledge is used to separate us from our money through marketing and advertising schemes appealing to these psychological nuances. Of course, this money that we lose through clever marketing is ultimately sapping our savings and investments.

We are also working against ourselves. Most of the time, we succumb to our wants even when we know that we cannot afford it. The act of buying can even be pleasurable in itself, regardless of the product. Think about the way you shop for food. Most people make at least a couple of impulse buys when they go to the supermarket. You do not need the product, but you buy it because you imagine yourself using it. You see a fresh baked apple pie and you picture your family gathered around the table enjoying it together. It may have only cost a few dollars, but, because it was not on your list, by purchasing the product you have raised the amount of money you spent on food that week. You may have even gotten the cheaper of the pies available to you, but the truth is you rationalized the extra purchase by buying the cheaper product. You had just bargained with yourself.

Sometimes you may even buy the more expensive product because you can't bring yourself to buy something generic or inferior. You construct such negative feelings with the generic product that you actually convince yourself to spend more, though in reality, you have no idea how good or bad that generic product was. You allowed uncertainty and fear to dictate your purchasing process. You may have imagined the disappointment that would result from the inferior product or maybe the social stigma that may result from giving a generic product to a friend or family member. Your emotions have just controlled your spending.

Stores and sales people have subtle ways of getting you to give in to those impulses. In a supermarket the brand name products (and more expensive products) are eye level and easy to access. The generics, on the other hand, are on the lowest shelf almost on the floor. The positioning and inconvenience of the generic product was designed to force you to buy the brand name.

Impulse buying is also influenced by something called decision fatigue. Psychologists have discovered that over the course of a long

THE RETIREMENT PITFALL

decision making process, people start to make worse decisions toward the end of the session. In a study by Roy F. Baumeister of Florida State University, two groups of college students were given a series of decisions between various items. One group was told that they would only keep one of the items they chose after a number of decisions, and the second group was asked to give their preferences on items with no final decisions between the products. After the test, both groups were asked to put a hand in ice water for as long as possible. The group that had made decisions with consequences was able to put their hands in the water for an average of 28 seconds, compared to 67 seconds for the second non-deciding/preference group. The conclusion that was reached was after having made all those decisions, the first group had lost a significant amount of will-power.[1] Other similar studies have shown the same trend to be true. As decisions begin piling up on someone, the tendency is to give up on making a decision more quickly, resulting in poorer choices. That is why after spending so much time making decisions in a supermarket, the check out aisles have candy and gum around them. All the decisions you have made in the store make it more likely that you will give in to your impulse at the last second and buy that Snickers Bar. This is also why you see so many options available to you at places like car dealerships. Before the dealer closes the sale, they attempt to give you as many decisions as possible. They offer the car in black or silver, coupe or sedan, manual or automatic. By the time you are ready to make the purchase, it is difficult to say no. That is also part of the reason you discuss financing after agreeing to buy. You've make so many decisions that you almost have to say yes to all the payment options coming your way.

The attempt to make a decision final before hearing details, is part of another strategy that sales people use to get you to buy their product. They know once someone has made a decision, they tend to stick to their guns. You will defend the decisions you have already made aggressively even in light of new negative details. The dealer will give you a number of easy decisions, which after added up, equals the car you want. After you have agreed upon the color, make, and model of the car, it is easier to have you buy even when you hear a price you dislike. It is difficult to say no to the price after you have said yes so many times to the car. It is also more difficult to refuse the financing terms because you have already become so emotionally invested in having and experiencing the car. In your mind you have already bought the car. You buy for emotional reasons.

Money's Understudy

The ways people spend their money can also affect their levels of spending. Businesses and banks have created clever ways for you to whittle those dollars away without really appreciating how much money you are actually spending. Fees and charges can sap you of cash, but by far the most dangerous trick people have devised to drain your bank accounts are devices that allow you to spend money without actually exchanging it; stand-ins for money. One of the most famous stand-ins for money is casino chips. Long ago, casino owners realized that it was much easier to get people to give their money to the house if what they were using to make bets did not look like money. Other businesses have caught on recently and have begun making their own stand-ins for money. Carnivals have tickets, arcades have tokens, and hotels can have you charge things to your room, all to make you feel like you aren't actually spending money. Even higher end businesses have begun to use stand-ins. Cruise lines offer their own credit cards that you fill up at the beginning of the trip. The idea is that in your mind you have already spent that money so you will try to get rid of all the money on the card before you disembark.

Banks and other institutions have also gotten in on the action and developed ways to make money easier to spend. Devices such as debit and credit cards create a layer of separation from you and your physical money, making it much easier to spend with the swipe of a card. Credit card spending has increased the amount Americans are willing to spend in various parts of their lives. In fact, a Dunn & Bradstreet study found that people spend 12-18% more when using credit cards than when using cash. McDonald's found that the aver-

◄ THE RETIREMENT PITFALL

age transaction rose from $4.50 to $7 when customers used plastic instead of cash.[2] The reasons for this change in behavior could be many. For one, using a credit card gives you instant access to a large amount of wealth. In the past, people would make the decision how much money to bring shopping. If they spent that amount, then they would have to wrestle with the unpleasant idea of going the bank to take more money out. Now with a card, you have the ability to spend to your credit limit and only pay back the minimum balance every month. What you conveniently don't take into account is the interest payments that you will have to pay down the road. Paying the minimum balance and getting hit with the interest fees on a credit card every month can wreak havoc on your finances. It is true that debit cards do not charge interest because the payments are coming out of your banking account, but debit cards do separate you from your money, which in turn makes it easier to spend.

Of course, if used responsibly, credit can have its advantages over cash.

- The most important thing to remember is that you must pay off the balance every month if you plan on using the card often. This allows you to access the convenience of a credit card without getting interest fees for it.
- You can track your finances better. Credit cards now have online features that will track every purchase you make for you. If you plan to use a credit card to buy most of the things you need, I would recommend learning to use these websites. They can tell you how much you are spending each month and break it down into sections such as gas and groceries so you can budget better.
- Credit Cards are also more secure. If your card is lost or stolen all it takes to cancel the card is a simple phone call. If you lose cash you're out of luck. Also, most cards offer incentives for using their card. Things like airline miles and cash back can really be useful if you pay your balance off every month.

The federal government has figured out ways to make you feel okay about spending money too. The one that everyone in the nation must deal with is income tax. The government has set up a system where they withhold your income in order to make sure that people pay their fair share come tax season. The problem is that normally after deductions; the government has taken too much money out of your pay. The way they give you back that money is in the form of a refund check. Most people cherish their refund check, but the fact is that refund checks are bad. If you receive a refund check that means that you are giving the government an interest free loan. That money could have been in your pocket and you could have used it much earlier to finance your retirement. If you are receiving a refund it may be time to review your W-4 withholding statement.

By increasing the number of personal allowances on your W-4 form you are asking the government to withhold less money. If you ask for less money to be withheld then there is less of a chance that you will receive a refund on your taxes. This means the money that would have previously went to the government is now going to you. Here's the catch. You can only ask for less withholding if certain life events occur. The most common of these life events are getting married or having children. If either of these events has happened and you have not updated your W-4, then you may be withholding too much for your taxes. Keep more money in your pocket to keep yourself out of debt or to finance your retirement. Make your money work for you, not the government. Be careful though; make sure you withhold enough money to pay your tax obligations. It is just as bad writing Uncle Sam a fat check at the end of the year if you withheld too little. The objective should be a tax refund of $0.

In For a Penny, In For a Pound

Another mistake Americans often make in regard to spending is spending too much money on very large and very small purchases. We overspend so often on small purchases that most of the time it probably slips right under our noses. You spend $15 on a martini in a bar in New York. How much do you think it cost to actually make that drink? You order room service at a fancy hotel. Do you think that hamburger was actually worth $20? You buy a beer and hot dog at a baseball park. How much do you think it cost to produce those items? Chances are the markup on those items are somewhere in the ballpark (pun intended) of 4 or 5 times the cost of the item. Since the amount is small we overcome the steep price of the item because we want instant gratification, but over the long haul these practices could cost you hundreds or thousands of dollars a year.

The same idea comes into play when making very large purchases. You finally built up the courage to buy that brand new $50,000 BMW you always dreamed of. As you're completing the final details of the sale, the dealer offers you 4-zone climate control and heated massage seats for an extra couple thousand. You've already spent $50,000. What difference is an additional $2,000 or $3,000 going to make? Your monthly payment may only go up an extra $50. Chances are you will be ready to deal with that after overcoming the initial $50,000 sticker shock. You have now spent an extra $3,000 for something you didn't even consider when you came in to buy. That is the danger of rationalizing a large purchase.

Inheritances

Some people may have the good fortune to retire lucky, but luck is what you make of it. Those counted among the lucky are a number of Baby Boomers that are retiring and are counting on some sort of family inheritance to fund their retirement in some way. As a whole, Baby Boomers are expected to receive an estimated $8.4 trillion in inheritances; they've gotten $2.4 trillion already with $6 trillion more on the way, according to the Center for Retirement Research at Boston College. That works out to a median amount of $64,000, an average of nearly $300,000 per inheriting household.[3] This is a ton of money, but you must be careful not to get those cartoon dollars signs in your eyes if you are inheriting. Inheritances often do not drastically alter your lifestyle, but if inheritances are used responsibly and rationally, they can definitely improve your long-term finances.

SPENDING/OLD HABITS

There are those stories of massive inheritances that take a poor working class family from living paycheck to paycheck to not having to ever worry about money again, but this is by far the exception and not the rule. Inheritances will normally have a larger impact on poorer families than it will on more wealthy ones, but it is up to you to make it life changing. If you come into an inheritance, the first thing you should do is take a step back and assess its value. What does it mean in terms of your real finances? How much will it add to your yearly retirement plan? Once you break down the inheritance into sections it is much easier to think about it rationally.

Inheritances can be a tricky asset for emotional reasons. Some heirs may become too attached to the money, and therefore make mistakes in its investment. If you are having trouble deciding what to do with the money initially, it is completely okay to take some time to think about its uses, but make sure you put the waiting money in something that is liquid and will earn you some returns while you think. Be sure to keep in mind that an inheritance is not income and will eventually run out if not properly managed, no matter what the amount.

When you do decide what to do with an inheritance, make sure it is for the right reasons. It may be hard to do anything with the money when you realize how hard your mother or father worked for it. However, that does not mean that they would want it to sit dormant in your checking account. They would probably be mad at you for that! Don't leave the money in the same account or the same stock in which it was given to you unless it makes financial sense. Your father may have made a mint on Microsoft stock, but that does not mean there aren't better places to invest. It is even more dangerous to keep money in an asset that is losing money simply for sentimental reasons. Make sure that the money they give you does not go to waste and that you take advantage of their generosity in a way that would make them proud. If they had wishes for the money, make sure that it fits with your financial plans. If their wishes were for you to buy a house that the extended family could vacation in together, make

◄ THE RETIREMENT PITFALL

sure that the inherited money could back up their wishes and that the money couldn't be used to benefit your family in a better way.

Be sure not to spend every last red cent of the inheritance either. If you do not have an emergency fund this would be an excellent time to create one. Keep 3-6 months worth of expenses in a liquid asset so that if times get tough, you have something that you can instantly access for no penalty. If you do plan on spending, make sure that you clean house a bit before you make any splurge purchases. Pay down your debt and get rid of monthly payments that dig into your earnings. You should pay off your car and any other personal loans, and if you can pay off your mortgage you should. That way you can stop paying interest and start seeing more of your paychecks or retirement funds. The only thing you may want to watch for is penalties for paying off your mortgage early. If that is the case, if you only pay off part of the mortgage, and therefore have a larger equity share of your house, you may get a lower interest rate if you refinance. That could save you thousands down the road.

If the inheritance is considerable and you are thinking long term with the money, it may be advantageous not to spend any of it. I do not mean do nothing with the money; I mean have the money work for you. You may be able to supplement your income considerably by putting the amount in an investment vehicle that pays interest or produces a consistent return. Every year you can simply skim the interest off the account and you'll never have to touch the principal. Have the interest from the inheritance pay off your monthly bills while you enjoy the income from your investments freely. If you are still working you could take the extra money to increase your contributions to your own retirement funds. Then you will add even more value to the inheritance and increase your nest egg for further financial stability.

If you inherit an IRA, there is a different set of rules to adhere to. Unlike a personal IRA, you cannot make a transfer from an inherited IRA to another retirement fund by withdrawing the money personally. The account must be transferred to another retirement fund through a trustee-to-trustee transfer, otherwise you could incur penalties. You may not mix the account with any of your own and the account must be identified as an inherited account. If you are not the spouse of the IRA owner, then you cannot treat the IRA as your own account. This means that the money will not be withdrawn according to your retirement schedule, or in other words you won't have the ability to wait until you are 70 ½ to begin taking money out of the account. When you receive the account you must begin taking Required Minimum Distributions (RMDs) by December 31st of the year following the year you received the account. You may continue taking the RMDs for the remainder of your expected life and still enjoy the benefits of the tax deferred (or tax free in the case of a Roth IRA) retirement account until you exhaust the principal. You may also liquidate the account and take a lump sum distribution if cash is needed quickly, though taxes may be heavy when claiming so much income all at once.

If you are the spouse of the owner of the account then you may treat the IRA as one of your own accounts. This means you may roll over the IRA to your own account and the required minimum distributions will not begin until you turn 70 ½. The obvious benefits are that the longer the money goes untouched in your tax deferred IRA, the more opportunity there is for growth of the account. If the account is already making RMDs, you can stop the payout if you are younger than 70 ½, but only if you are the spouse and treat the account as yours.

There are certain scenarios where keeping the account in the deceased's name may be beneficial; at least for a little while. Let us assume that a husband dies before 70 ½ and leaves an IRA to his wife who is younger than 59 ½. She may want to hold onto the account unchanged in order to be able to access it before she is 59 ½ and avoid the 10% early withdrawal fees she would encounter if the account was in her name. If the husband is younger than 70 ½, she will not have to pay RMDs until the husband would have reached that age. The wife can then transfer her spouse's IRA to her name when she reaches 59 ½ in order to prevent RMDs until she is 70 ½. Again, even if the wife has begun paying RMDs on her husband's account before rolling it over, it is still completely okay to stop the RMDs by transferring the account to her name. Keeping the account unchanged early on would afford the spouse the ability to withdraw from the account penalty free before they are 59 ½ when the account is under her older husband's name. Later on, changing the account avoids RMDs that would suck value out of the account and allows the wife to pull from the account without penalty now that she is 59 ½. If your head is spinning it's okay. That's quite common. When you inherent something like an IRA or some other sort of complex investment vehicle it is always best to consult a financial professional. Everyone's circumstances are different; give your situation the attention it deserves in order to maximize the effectiveness of your gift.

One last word about inheritances and one last piece of crucial advice: If you don't have it, don't count on it. Many people know (or assume) that their parents or their relatives are rich and powerful and that they will grace them with the gift of their wealth. Never plan for an inheritance; it is assuming something that is almost completely beyond your control. Make sure that you have the financial stability and ability to survive without the additional income. Imagine the impact an inheritance will have to your finances if it is seen as a boon or a windfall instead of a necessity. As much as they may love you, you never truly know what plans your parents and relatives have for their money. Take responsibility for your retirement. Don't rely on inheritances.

How Can You Improve Your Bad Spending Habits?

While reading this chapter you may have caught some bad spending habits that you have. Thankfully it is never too late to change. Practice the following money saving strategies in order to save more for your retirement.

- <u>Make a Retirement Budget</u> – Make sure that you write out your budget. Keep an Excel spreadsheet or QuickBooks in order to construct a coherent and easy to change budget platform. Be honest about what kind of money you have available to you and work out a realistic budget for yourself. Do not try to work out your budget in your head. When you try to work out your budget in your head things can get unnecessarily complicated. What if you overspend? Will you mentally increase the amount spent in one area of your budget and take that spending away in another? That will get confusing really fast. Make yourself a hard copy budget and do not deviate from it as much as possible.

- Refrain From Using Credit Irresponsibly – Do not keep a high interest balance on a credit card. Unless you pay off your credit card completely every month, try to use cash for your day to day purchases. It's harder to spend cash and chances are you won't want to go get more if you run out. Make sure that if at all possible you do not take out your credit card. Use credit for things that there is not an opportunity to overspend on. Things like the energy bill and the cable bill. Places like restaurants are bad places to use credit because there spending can quickly get out of control.
- When You Do Have To Buy, Make a List - Do not get anything not on the list. You can further refine your list and separate needs from wants if you are really running a tight budget. That way once you hit your spending limit, you know what you can do without.
- Shop Alone – Shopping with friends can be fun but there may be some peer pressure involved there. If your friend is buying something, you may want to impress him or her and buy as well. Even worse, your friend may want to shop vicariously through you and run up your tab instead of theirs. Stick to your budget.
- Don't Tempt Yourself – Don't go to a place where you know you are going to spend money. If you like electronics and you're on a budget; it would probably be a bad idea to wander aimlessly through a Best Buy. Also, when you go grocery shopping eat before you go. Impulse will take over if you don't.

◄ **THE RETIREMENT PITFALL**

- <u>Keep Your Deductibles and Your Insurance Rates Reasonable</u> – Low deductibles may seem nice on paper, but it may mean much bigger payments every month to the insurance provider. This money could be going toward a retirement account instead of disappearing into premium payments. It may be wiser to keep your deductible high and keep that money instead. Also, make sure your insurances cover what you need them to cover. It's amazing how often people have insurance on things that they don't do and therefore don't need. Review your policies and make sure they work for you. If they don't, trim the fat and cut the coverage that is dead weight.
- <u>Refinance and Renegotiate Your Bills</u> – Chances are you're going to have a tough time renegotiating something like your mortgage in order to keep your spending down, but refinancing may be an option. If refinancing would lower your monthly payment, determine at what point you would begin making money. For instance, if refinancing would save you $100 on your monthly payment and closing costs are $5000, you would have to live in your house for 4 years and 2 months in order to break even and have the refinancing be worthwhile. Make sure you do the math and plan on owning the house for a while if you plan on saving money this way.
- <u>There are also other parts of your finances that are more forgiving.</u> Medical institutions such as doctors and hospitals are normally very understanding and will forgive some of your medical bills. In fact, around 60% of doctors will forgive at least some medical bills, and those savings could be as much as 25% in some cases. If you don't like negotiating there are paid medical advocates that will take a percentage of the savings and negotiate your bills for you.[4] Also, companies like phone and cable providers will often change their rate in order to keep you as a customer. If your bill goes from $100 to $80 a month, that's a yearly savings of $240. This money is a small savings that could go into your IRA.

- Keep a Reasonable Emergency Fund – Keeping too much money in a bank account could be bad for a number of reasons. First of all, money in checking and savings accounts are hardly making any money. In fact, this money is being eaten up by inflation. These dollars could be working much harder for you in your retirement accounts. It is important to have a savings account to fall back on, but most financial planners agree that three to six months of salary is an acceptable amount to have in reserve. Keep in mind that bank accounts are FDIC insured, whereas both principal and yield of investment securities do have risk and may fluctuate with changes in market conditions.
- Keeping a modest amout of money in your bank account – If your account becomes too large it will make your payments out of the account seem small, and your tendency will be to spend more money because of it. Would it be easier to take $1000 out of an account with a total of $5000 or $100,000? Keeping a modest amout of money in your bank account will keep you from throwing your money away by letting you see the impact of your spending.
- Make Sure You Know What You Want – Do you need the latest phone or the finest cars? If you spend now you will pay later. The more money spent on luxury before you retire means the less money you will have when you retire. Keep goals for your retirement and attach realistic savings amounts to those goals. That way if you begin to waver in your saving habits, you have a number that can help you refocus on your retirement objectives.

When it comes to spending, it may very well be a hard habit to break. We live in a hyper-consumer society and everything around you is constantly begging for your dollars. To avoid this constant pressure, take yourself away from temptation. Try to imagine yourself ten years from now and what you would want for yourself in the future. Make goals and attach realistic values to those goals. Then

◄ THE RETIREMENT PITFALL

you can begin budgeting to reach what you want. Don't be a slave to your emotions and bad habits, practice discipline and control your spending.

CHAPTER 3 ENDNOTES

1. Teirney, John. "Do You Suffer From Decision Fatigue?" The New York Times Aug 17 2011. Web.
2. "New Year's Resolutions: 7 for Your Money." *CBSNews*. CBS Interactive, 06 Dec. 2010. Web. 27 Mar. 2012. <http://www.cbsnews.com/8301-505144_162-41541152/new-years-resolutions-7-for-your-money/>.
3. *Forbes*. "How To Make the Most of Your Inheritance" Forbes Magazine. Web. 28 Mar. 2012. <http://www.forbes.com/2011/02/15/baby-boomers-retirement-how-to-make-the-most-of-your-inheritance.html>.
4. "How to Negotiate Your Medical Bills." *DailyFinance.com*. Web. 02 Apr. 2012. <http://www.dailyfinance.com/2010/05/21/how-to-negotiate-your-medical-bills/>.

CHAPTER 4

Investments

"When a possibility is unfamiliar to us, we do not even think about it."
– Nate Silver

WHILE IT IS important to keep from losing your money by avoiding mistakes and controlling your spending, it is equally important that you continue to grow your money through sound investing. In order to invest soundly, it is important that you have a well rounded financial education so good decisions can be made. Therefore, I would be remiss if I didn't let you in on the general must knows of investing. Some of these tips are for general investing and some may be more useful for retirement investing, but I feel that you deserve to know all the important details. Now the first thing you should know is that having investment knowledge isn't about beating the market, it's about preparedness. Knowing about the various forms of investing will not always allow you to avoid taking a loss or have you make amazing gains, but it will help you understand what to do if you find yourself in those positions.

Stay Cool

In the late 14th and early 15th century, the Ottoman Turks introduced Europe to the beauty that is the tulip. The Dutch were especially fond of tulips and they began to grow their own. Because tulips were

THE RETIREMENT PITFALL

beautiful and new at the time they fetched a high price in European markets. While the tulip was in Europe, it contracted a disease called Mosaic. This disease caused all sorts of wonderful patterns on the petals of the flower, which added to its aesthetic beauty and further inflated the price of a tulip bulb.

A number of Dutchman began to see opportunity in the tulip. Bulb buyers began to stockpile bulbs, which lowered the amount of bulbs available for sale and artificially inflated the price. Soon tulips were in such high demand and so expensive that people were foolishly selling their homes or squandering their life savings in order to get a bulb. The Dutch believed that foreigners would not know the true value of a tulip and would buy the plant at vastly inflated prices while they would reap enormous profits. Obviously, the price the Dutch were offering was not rational and no one would buy a simple flower for such an outrageous price. Some Dutch realized that continuing to hold the bulbs was dangerous and sold their bulbs early to make a profit. The selling caused the price of tulips to fall which in turn caused a chain reaction of frantic selling by bulb buyers afraid of holding the bulbs until they were worthless. As prices continued to drop panic set in and people began to sell their tulip bulbs at significant losses. At the end of the crisis, many people were financially ruined because they had thrown away their whole life savings on a plant. An economic depression ensued that damaged the entire Dutch economy.

The lesson here is that it's important that you act rationally when you are investing, because the market not always is. The Dutch tulip bubble may have happened almost 500 years ago, but it can still teach us about economic bubbles today. Be careful about following trends. If something seems too good to be true, it likely is.

In 2012, the United States is recovering from its own investment bubble. The landscapes of finance and investment are still marred with the scars of the housing crisis of 2008 and the recession that followed. A modest recovery has followed in the past couple of years. Some people are still nervous about the stock market and the economy in general and remember the losses that they may have taken only a few years earlier. Almost everyone lost money, but some have backed out of investing, cementing the losses they endured; while others have weathered the storm and are on the road to recovery. This does not mean that the latter group is better than the former group at investing; they just know an important lesson about investing: Don't be emotional with your investing and know where you are going.

Know Your Objectives

When making any investment, it is essential to know what you want from your investments and what risks you are willing to take before you buy.

When starting young, retirement is typically a long term investment. Most investors agree that when investing long term, a portfolio can handle greater risk. This is because over time, higher risk investments tend to outperform their lower risk counterparts. Therefore, those that are younger can stand to have a greater amount of higher risk investments such as equities in their portfolio.

However, every retirement is different. Take into account how far you want to go and how fast you need to get there. It may be easy to walk a mile in 15 minutes, but it is much more difficult to walk a mile in 5 minutes. If you are approaching retirement, have a shorter time frame available to make a gain, or are in more immediate need for money, it is often better to have investments that offer less risk such as ones that guarantee the return of your principal, even though returns on these investments might be more modest.

If your time frame to retirement is flexible, it may allow a bit more experimentation than if you have a set schedule you must meet. If you are planning to retire early but it is not absolutely necessary to retire at that age, you may have the option to slightly increase your risk in hopes that your investments perform favorably and you are able to meet your goal early. However, you must be aware that when you increase your risk there is always the chance of your investments doing badly and that ultimately the poor performance of your investments may move you farther from your goal.

◄ **THE RETIREMENT PITFALL**

If you're approaching retirement age that probably means that you will have to reevaluate the direction that your investments are currently moving in. Typically in retirement your most important objective is to find a way to use the money you currently have now for the next 20 or 30 years of your life. Most do this by lowering their investment risk, and making their money easier to access, both of which I will detail later in the chapter.

When you reach retirement it is also important that you do not react emotionally to things like market crashes and sacrifice your objectives. In 2008 some people did react emotionally when the market took a huge hit. Those are the people that pulled their money out when the market was low and crystallized their losses. Those that kept their money in may well be on the road to recovery now. Who do you think made the wiser decision? When investing you should always be patient and pay attention to the full picture.

Securities

Before we get into how to construct and mange an investment portfolio we should quickly detail the assets that are commonly used in today's markets.

STOCKS

Stocks are a form of equity security that allows the holder of the stock to partake in the profits and failures of the company they are part of. Stocks also allow a shareholder to influence the management of a company by using their stock voting rights to help elect people to the company's board of directors.

Most stocks share these general attributes, but market analysts have attempted to break them down further based on the size and behavior of the stock. The first way that analysts do this is by looking at the stocks market capitalization. Market capitalization is calculated by taking the total outstanding shares the company has on the market and multiplying that by the value of the stock. Stocks with a total value over $10 billion are considered a large-cap stocks, mid-cap stocks are

INVESTMENTS

between $10 billion and $2 billion, and stocks valued under $2 billion are small cap stocks. The most well known large-cap stocks that have a good history and reputation are known as blue chip stocks. Generally speaking, blue chips are considered a less risky investment than other stock investments. Normally, the less market capitalization a stock has, the more risky the stock is.

Stocks are categorized by the way they behave as well.

- Growth Stocks - Stocks that have quickly growing earnings which they reinvest back into the company are called growth stocks. These stocks have the potential to appreciate quickly, but they are riskier than most other stock categories. They also rarely pay dividends.
- Income Stocks – Income stocks pay higher than average dividends to their investors. People that are in need of immediate income will often invest in these stocks. Keep in mind though, dividends are subject to change and are not guaranteed.
- Defensive Stocks – These stocks tend to stay strong even when the economy is not doing that well. These stocks tend to be in market sectors such as food and pharmaceuticals that sell steadily despite changes in the market. While these stocks tend not to fall much during a bear market, they also tend not to rise much during a bull market.
- Cyclical Stocks – These stocks tend to be companies that produce items people buy a lot of during good times and do not buy during bad economic times such as cars and travel. These stocks typically rise and fall with the economy.

The main advantage of owning stock is the potential for long term capital appreciation. Though they have misbehaved in the recent past, historically stocks have outperformed all other types of securities. If the market on the whole is doing well or if the company is well managed, stock appreciation is possible. Stocks also have the advantage of being subject to capital gains taxation. Any increase in value between the time you have bought a stock and the time you have sold a stock is a capital gain. As of the year 2012, the long term capital gains rate is

◄ THE RETIREMENT PITFALL

15%, which is considerably lower than most earned income tax rates.

While stocks do tend to appreciate more significantly than other securities in the long run, they are subject to the highest volatility of any of the asset classes. Because of this, stocks are not appropriate for investment situations where you may need your investment in a short period of time. Stocks also subject the investor to a higher amount of risk than other possible investments. The possibility of gains also means the possibility of losses.

BONDS

Bonds are different from stocks because they are debt securities, which means when you own a bond the company that you bought the bond from owes you money and will pay you interest for it. When the term of a bond is up, the company promises to return the principal of the loan back to you.

With a stock there is no promise by the company to pay stockholders back in the event that the company does not do well. You are partial owner of a company, and you make and lose money with the success or failure of the company. This difference in ownership typically makes bonds a less risky investment, though the chances for appreciation are generally lower than stocks.

Bonds are normally sold in increments of $1000, which is called their par value and the company pays its bond back at an interest rate called the coupon rate. Once a bond is purchased, the market price of a bond is normally determined by changes in interest rates. If the interest rate for new bonds from the same issuer moves above the coupon rate of your bond, your bond will sell at a discount on the market. Conversely, if those interest rates move below your bond's coupon rate that makes your bond attractive to investors and your bond will sell for more than its par value on the market.

Bonds are sold by corporations to fund their operations, but many bonds are also sold by the U.S. Government to raise money for its operations as well. U.S. government securities come in a variety of formats that are appropriate for all kinds of different investment strategies. They are often considered some of the safest investments since they are backed by the full faith and credit of the U.S. Government and it's highly unlikely that the government would ever default on its obligations. U.S. securities are highly liquid and they hold an advantage over other bond issues because they are exempt from state and local taxes all over the United States. Local governments also issue their own bonds called municipal bonds. Municipal bonds are typically triple tax exempt, meaning you do not have to pay federal, state, or local taxes on them if you are a resident of the state of issuance, though they may be subject to the Alternative Minimum Tax (AMT).

The main advantage that bonds hold over other securities such as stocks is that they are more predictable. If you hold a bond you know exactly how much interest you will receive, and those interest rates typically exceed what you will get from other accounts that pay interest such as savings accounts. With bonds you also know you will get your principal back, unless the company defaults on your loan. People that are hesitant to engage in the risk of stocks often turn to bonds because they offer a way to have a more secure source of income.

However, bonds do have their drawbacks. First bonds don't offer the possibility of high yield returns like stocks. If you are okay with risk and have an acceptable time period to make an investment, a stock may be a better choice to help reduce inflation risk. Also, if you get a long term bond and the interest rates go up after you have made your purchase, you now have your money tied up an investment that is not making you as much money as bonds are in the current market. This will devalue the sale price of your bond, making it unattractive to sell. Finally, if the bond issuer goes bankrupt you have the possibility of losing your investment or getting a reduced value for your bond.

Mutual Funds

In order to have a successful portfolio, most professional investors recommend that you make sure your investments are well diversi-

---

*Diversification does not assure a profit or protect against a loss.

◄ THE RETIREMENT PITFALL

fied.* The problem that many investors have is that in order to be properly diversified, you have to invest a good amount of money into many different assets. This often proves difficult for the average investor just looking to build a retirement or supplement their income. In order to make diversification available to people other than the wealthy, investment companies created the mutual fund. The mutual fund allows investors to pool resources and invest in a vast array of securities to achieve portfolio diversity.

Mutual funds are diversified, but they also normally have a specific investment objective such as growth or income. To keep the fund on track, the investment companies that construct these mutual funds assign a fund manager to make sure that the objectives of the fund are maintained. The fact that mutual funds have a professional managing your portfolio is attractive to some investors that cannot afford to hire a manager or learn the market on their own. This gives you professional management of your stock portfolio at a fraction of the price that it would cost otherwise. Because mutual funds are managed and maintained, mutual funds also take care of a lot of the bookkeeping that is associated with investing, making it a very convenient investment. Fund managers have constructed countless types of mutual funds to meet all types of investment objectives. If you can imagine an investment scenario, chances are there is a mutual fund to meet that need.

Another plus of mutual funds is that they are liquid. Instead of having to put your stocks on the market, mutual funds will buy back from you directly, making it very easy to redeem your shares. However, you are not able to redeem mutual fund shares until the end of the trading day when the fund's value is calculated.

Mutual funds do suffer some deficiencies. Like all securities based products, mutual funds have a certain degree of investment risk. The shares of mutual funds, when redeemed, may be worth more or less than their original value, meaning that your principal is not guaranteed and you may suffer a loss with the product. Also, although you may see professional management of your assets as a major plus for mutual funds, those managers must get paid. That means there are fees involved in mutual funds that you would not encounter if you invested in the stock market yourself. These fees have the potential to eat your profits if the fund is poorly managed. Mutual funds also suffer from dilution. This means that a fund may hold one very well performing stock, but that stock may represent a very small fraction of the funds overall holdings. The average performance of other stocks in the fund could dilute the gains of that one good stock.

Most investors choose mutual funds for the diverse options that they provide the investor, along with the ease of owning one. If you are interested in buying any investment product, be sure that you review the prospectus that will be given to you when you are introduced to it. The prospectus will discuss the performance of the investment over the last couple years and will reveal any fees associated with the product. Be a smart investor and do your homework before making any purchase.

Managing Your Investments

Asset Allocation

When you have decided on an objective to reach for your investments, you should only take as much risk as necessary to get there. For example, a simple portfolio may hold stocks, bonds, and cash equivalents such as money market funds. These three assets could be mixed in a number of ways, and there are probably a number of ways to get the growth potential you need in the time period necessary. However, reaching your goal in the time period desired is only half the battle. It is also important to expose yourself to the least amount of risk possible so you do not experience a large loss while attempting your objective. The trick is finding the mix of assets that will give the most efficient outcome.

The way that most portfolio managers do this is through asset allocation. After determining your current investments, your goals, and the risk you are willing to take to get where you want to be you need

THE RETIREMENT PITFALL

to find a mix of investments that fits your taste. Let's use an example to illustrate. Let's say you have portfolio that is invested 50% in stocks and 50% in bonds with an expected return of 9%. Using an asset allocation program you may find that your current asset mix is not the best for your objectives. There may be to two ways to optimize its performance. Maybe you are comfortable with the amount of risk that you have. If you would like to increase your gains you may be able to do so with a change in assets that will not change the amount of risk in the portfolio, thereby making your investments more efficient. On the other hand, maybe you are comfortable with the amount of money you are making in gains already. If that's the case then there may be a way to lower your risk using asset allocation while maintaining the same expected gains.

Like any financial model, asset allocation is only as good as the data that it is based on. Normally, firms use the last couple decades of stock market data as a predictor of how the market will be in the future, but those predictions are certainly no guarantee. If you think that there is a different time period that more accurately reflects the future of the market you can plug those years into an asset allocation program to see what results you get. Asset allocation also requires a certain degree of maintenance as well. If part of your portfolio begins to outperform the rest of your investments that may change the balance of securities that you have and ruin your strategy. Asset allocation requires rebalancing from time to time to ensure the strategy remains effective.

The typical diversified portfolio invests in different types of stocks, bonds, money market funds, and mutual funds. However, this portfolio may not truly be diversified. In order for a portfolio to be diversified it must be diversified between asset classes (stocks, bonds, etc.) and must be diversified within those assets classes. You have to see what industries and what companies your stocks, bonds, and funds are invested in. If the assets classes in your portfolio are diverse, but if you had all of these assets invested in one sector, such as the tech industry, that would not be proper diversification. If the tech industry were to suddenly tank, you would be in for a world of hurt, no matter what form of tech investment you have. So not only do the types of assets you have need to be diverse, but the industries you are in must be diverse as well. To properly diversify, try to invest in industries that move in opposite directions when the economy moves and have little to do with each other. That way even in a down economy you are able to limit your risk.

Another strategy that is employed to diversify is geographic diversification. Sometimes different parts of the country are doing better economically than others. If you have assets that are located all over the country, a depression in one area may be softened by prosperity in another. This is also true of the global market. A weak economy in Europe may be offset by a boom in China. Having assets all over the world may serve to protect your investments. However, with international investing, there are special risk considerations involved, including currency fluctuations, lower liquidity, economic and political risk, and differences in accounting methods.

You may also want to diversify your investment portfolio with things other than stocks and bonds. One alternative that most people can easily begin investing in is commodities. Commodities are independent from paper assets but are traded in the market. Some view commodities like gold as a hedge against stocks and bonds because when the economy does poorly investors often run to these assets for protection. Please note that commodities tend to be extremely volatile and may be affected by overall market movements and other factors that affect the value of a particular industry or commodity, such as weather, disease, embargoes, or political and regulatory developments. They are not suitable for all investors.

Real estate is another investment that is consistently overlooked by many investors. Say you buy an investment property with a 15 year mortgage. Yes that is certainly a liability. However, if you find a tenant to cover the mortgage you now have someone buying a house for you. If you consistently get tenants for the next 15 years you could own a piece of property while having essentially paid no money for it. After the house is paid off you have an income stream that will pay for as long as you hold onto the property and you will be able to raise rent with the pace of inflation. That could be an excellent retirement plan!

You may have experimented with these different investments from time to time throughout your life or you may not have. Either way, it is never too late to get in the game and try to diversify. Remember if you are not properly diversified, a bad turn in the economy can lay your portfolio to waste. If you are fully diversified in different types of assets then you may be able to make money even while the market is down. Remember though, diversification cannot guarantee a profit or protect against a loss.

Tax Diversification

You always hear about having asset diversification, but even having different assets in different sectors of the economy does not mean you are fully diversified. When investing, and especially when investing for retirement, it is important that you achieve tax diversification as well. Being tax diversified means that the assets that you hold are not all the same in terms of when you must pay tax on them. This strategy is a benefit especially for retirees because not being taxed on all of their withdrawals from their retirement accounts can save them from jumping up in tax brackets and therefore paying a higher percentage of their savings to tax.

There are three types of taxable assets that you can have:
- Taxable accounts
- Tax deferred accounts
- Tax free accounts

With a taxable account the story is the same as any other investment account. You put money into the account and that money is considered your cost basis. Any gains that you make in the account will be taxed at either short term or long term capital gains rates depending on how long you have held the account. A normal brokerage account that holds stock would be an example of a taxable account.

INVESTMENTS

Taxed deferred accounts are different because they allow you to put money into an account before you pay tax. The account is then allowed to grow tax deferred. You finally pay tax on the account when you make a withdrawal on the account and you are taxed on the entire amount you withdraw. An excellent example of a tax deferred account would be a 401(k) or a traditional IRA account. However, the positives or of the tax deferred traditional IRA come with the fact that withdrawals from a traditional IRA may be subject to a 10% penalty if taken prior to age 59 ½.

A tax free account is an account where you make the investment using money that has already been taxed. The gains in the account are then allowed to grow tax free. When you withdraw from such an account you do not have to pay any tax. A good example of a tax free account is a Roth IRA. Please be aware, in order to qualify for the tax free penalty free withdrawal of earnings, a Roth IRA must be in place for a least five years, and the distribution must take place after 59 ½.

Now the question that people often ask themselves when they are designing a retirement portfolio is are they taxed more now or will they be taxed more during retirement. If you think you are paying more tax now than you will be in the future, then a taxed deferred account would be the best option for you. If you believe you will be taxed more later, then a tax free account may be a better option.

The problem is that you really don't know if you will be taxed more now or later, especially if tax rates change. The solution to this uncertainty is spreading out your tax risk or tax diversifying. This way you can't be caught off guard if anything happens in your life to significantly change your tax status or if there are changes in tax law down the road. Just like putting all your money in stocks could be a disaster if the stocks do not do well, putting all your money in tax deferred investments could be a disaster if you end up in a higher tax bracket after you retire. Unless you are absolutely sure on the tax bracket you will be in when you retire, hedge your bets and spread out your tax obligations.

◄ THE RETIREMENT PITFALL

Knowing When to Buy and Sell

Most people are familiar with the cyclical movements of the economy and the business cycle from decline to prosperity, or vice versa. Knowing the business cycle is good, but knowing how to apply the knowledge of the cycle to how you make investment decisions can give you an edge in your portfolio.

Most people are emotional when it comes to money, not only in their spending but also in their investments. When people see an investment doing well, most will watch in the beginning. Most non-professional investors need a lot of convincing evidence for them to invest, so they wait for the investment to show greater gains until they finally buy. However, they have just committed the first sin of the investing cycle. Often an investment that has highly performed for a while has already hit its growth spurt. It then may very well hit the next step of the business cycle: its decline. Many of those investors that bought at the height of the investment will continue to hold it, hoping that their fortunes will change only to see it fall further until they sell, disgusted with their decision. The decline may end up only being a fraction of the gains that the investment made, but to the investors that bought at the height of the investment; this decline could be a considerable loss.

These investors have made a mistake that many amateur investors make: buying when the market is high. In fact, this mistake is so common that there are fund managers on Wall Street that actually will do the opposite of what misinformed investors do, assuming that it is inherently the right decision. Do not allow yourself to fall victim to your emotions, know how to think rationally about the market.

You should resist the urge to get caught up in the hype of an over performing investment and should resist the urge to panic and sell when your investment is down. When you think a business or sector of the economy has bottomed out, that may be a good time for you to buy. If you see an investment performing well, be careful not to jump on the bandwagon too late. Especially as a retiree don't get antsy when investing. Retirement investing should be about security and your long term well being. Have patience and your results could look a lot better.

Dollar Cost Averaging

One school of thought about the buying of securities is dollar cost averaging. It is especially effective at removing emotion and fear from the buying process. Dollar cost averaging is done by investing a set amount of money in an investment at a regular interval regardless of the investment's performance. Dollar cost averaging works because although the amount of money invested remains the same, the value of the investment is constantly changing. For instance, if you invest $100 in a stock that is $20 in week 1 you have bought 5 shares of the underlying investment. In week 2 you invest the same $100, but this time the stock has dropped to $10. Though the drop in price is bad for your existing stock, because the price has dropped, you were able to buy more stock in week 2 for the same price you paid in week 1. This strategy works because you end up buying more shares when the stock is low which will lower the average cost of the stock over time. Dollar cost averaging also removes the stress of having to time the market or keep close watch on your investments. Investing a small amount before a dip in the market is no big deal. Investing your life savings and immediately taking a 20% hit could give you a heart attack!

The best thing to invest in with dollar cost averaging is something that takes fees proportional to the investment being made. For instance, some investment accounts charge a flat transaction fee regardless of the amount of money being traded. This type of account would not be best for dollar cost averaging because when you are using this strategy you are making many small transactions and you would be charged a flat fee on each trade. Other investments like some mutual funds will charge a transaction fee proportional to the amount of money being traded. This type of account would be better for dollar cost averaging because, even with small trades, the account would only charge a small fraction of the total trade being executed.

◄ THE RETIREMENT PITFALL

This means instead of being hit with a $10 fee for any transaction you make, you may have to pay 0.3% of your contribution in fees. If your contributions are small you'll be saving a ton of money.

The one problem with dollar cost averaging is that it is a long-term strategy and it may take a while to get a considerable portfolio started with it. It also takes time for dollar cost averaging to work because it takes time for the prices of most investments to change significantly. If you make 10 purchases in the course of a month, it will likely do little to change the average cost of your investment. If you make a purchase once a month over a year, you have a much better chance of dollar cost averaging being effective because the price of the investment has probably changed over that time period. If you have a small time window dollar cost averaging may take too much time to make any real investment progress. If you are age 50 and are looking to get a new portfolio started dollar cost averaging may be a good way to start. If you're age 70 it may be time to make bigger decisions about your investments. Please note dollar cost averaging does not assure a profit or protect against a loss in declining markets. Such a plan involves continuous investment in securities regardless of the fluctuating price levels of the securities and the investor should consider his or her financial ability to continue purchases through periods of low levels.

USE YOUR LOSSES TO OFFSET YOUR GAINS

Taking a loss on an investment is never fun, but in today's economy some investments are not as stable as they used to be. However, if you do have to take a loss in an investment account there is a silver lining to losing your money. Typically taxes can take a large part of any investment gains you make, but you may be able to use any losses you encounter to protect the gains you make in other investments. Every year the government allows you to claim $3,000 in investment losses and use those losses to offset any profits. The concept is called tax loss harvesting and is commonly used by investors to protect any gains they have made in the market.

INVESTMENTS

For instance, if you took a $6,000 loss in an investment in 2012, but made a $10,000 gain in another investment in the same year you will be able to offset $3,000 of that $10,000 gain and only pay capital gains on the remaining $7,000. Another good thing about reporting losses is that the extra $3,000 in losses that you did not report in 2012 can be rolled over and be used to offset any gains that you make in 2013 as well. This strategy allows you to minimize the effect of your losses by saving tax on your gains, thereby softening the blow of a bad investment and enhancing the good investment decisions that you have made.

One thing to keep in mind about tax loss harvesting is that it is used in brokerage accounts and not retirement accounts. Tax loss harvesting does not apply to investments like IRAs and 401(k)s. So don't go selling your retirement accounts trying to tax harvest!

Inflation

One of the best reasons to keep your money in securities when retiring is the fact that money that is sitting in your home and money that is in your bank account will not keep pace with inflation. That means your dollars are becoming worth less day by day. Stocks typically do keep pace with the rate of inflation in the long run, but if all you are looking for from your investment is inflation protection then a stock is an unnecessarily high risk.

If you want to preserve the buying power of your money but do not want to subject your money to high risk investments then you may want to invest in things designed to pace inflation. A good example of a security that is built for this type of investing is Treasury Inflation Protected Securities or TIPS. TIPS do not have a high rate of return, but they have the security of a government bond with the added bonus of inflation protection.

Investing For Income

When you reach retirement age, most people's thoughts turn from making money in the market to finding ways to turn those retirement

THE RETIREMENT PITFALL

accounts into something that provides security. The worst thing that you can do is build a retirement nest egg and then lose a large chunk of it because you were still too concerned with gains. If you want to preserve your wealth, tone down your risk.

Additionally, the gains you make in investing will not mean as much unless you have a plan as to how you are going to make those gains last. Some people accomplish this by using income investments. Income investments work for many retirement investors because they may help to preserve your principal while still having money coming in to fund your retirement.

There are a number of investments that are considered income producing investments:

- Dividend Paying Stocks – These are stocks that distribute a portion of their profits to their shareholders instead of re-investing the money in the company and driving the stock price up. Dividends are paid per share, so your payout will be based on the amount of shares that you own. If you want to invest in these types of stocks find companies they pay a large part of their profits to the shareholders through dividends. A dividend yield of about 5% of your stock price is a pretty good rate. Please be aware that dividends are subject to change and are not guaranteed.
- Bonds – Most bonds pay you a set rate of interest every year. Bonds will lock up the principal you invest in them unless you decide to sell the bond on the market, where bond prices will be determined by current interest rates and the creditworthiness of the issuer. If sold prior to maturity, a bond may be subject to a substantial gain or loss. Remember, as interest rates rise, bond prices fall.
- Annuities – Annuities are long term investment vehicles designed for retirement purposes that provide you with guaranteed income based on the amount of money that you have given to the account. These guarantees are based on the claims- paying ability of the insurance company. Annuities

give you the assurance that money will be coming in every month as long as the company that provides the annuity stays in business and is able to pay claims. Keep in mind that annuities generally come with fees and expenses that may not be present in other investments. Additionally, earnings withdrawn from an annuity are subject to ordinary income tax rates.
- Retirement Income Funds – Some mutual funds are specially designed to provide income for retirement. The good thing about retirement income funds is that if you don't like the fund you still have access to your money and can take it out whenever you want.
- Rental Property – Owning property and renting it can provide a stable source of income. The down side is that real estate does sometimes have unexpected costs. However, if you know what you are doing you can make good money.
- Real Estate Investment Trusts – REITs are investment companies that own and manage properties, collect rent from tenants, and pay for the necessary expenses of running a real estate investment. Though the profits may not be as good as owning your own properties, the inconvenience of managing the properties is left to the trust. REITs may not be appropriate for all investors. Certain REITs may have limited transferability and lack liquidity. The value of an investment in a REIT may fluctuate based on economic, regulatory and environmental factors. The value of the units or shares of the trust will fluctuate with the portfolio of the underlying real estate properties. Redemption may be at a price, which is more or less than the original price paid for the units by the investor.

Making the right investments is an important part of having a healthy portfolio and ultimately having a good enough nest egg to begin retirement. Always remember that retirement investing is a long term strategy and that quick fixes and large risks are not the answer

◄ **THE RETIREMENT PITFALL**

to retirement problems. Stay consistent and make sure that what you have worked so hard for continues to be cared for with smart and prudent investing.

CHAPTER 5

Financial Planning for Retirement

"If you don't know where you are going, any road will get you there."
  – Lewis Carroll

THUS FAR, WE have learned to overcome our fear, fix our retirement mistakes, and manage our spending. We have also talked about not having a plan and the stresses it can cause as you prepare for retirement. Like a house, your financial plan needs a strong foundation to be successful. Also, like a house, in order to build that foundation you will need a good blueprint to show the way. In this Chapter, we will talk about the methods you should use to formulate a plan and present the ways to set up a blueprint that will transform your finances into a coherent strategy to help yield real results.

Many people are not adequately prepared for retirement, which for many turns out to be a considerable chunk of their life. A number of retirees think that if they have investments like a 401(k) or an IRA that means that they have planned for their retirement. They will often ask me "Where should I put my money?" However, there is much more that can be done to fully prepare for retirement than simply opening an IRA. The real questions that they should be asking are "What strategy should I have when I make my investments?" and "How should I spend my money?" Retirement planning is more than

◄ **THE RETIREMENT PITFALL**

the investments accounts that you own. You need a plan. If you don't know your objective, how do you expect to get there? You need to know what you want to get it.

Step 1: Determine What You Have and What You Want

Everyone has a different financial situation going into retirement. Some people have been successful in saving a vast amount of wealth, and some have not been as fortunate. Some people are very good at saving and fiscal discipline; others seem to have money slip right through their fingers, always wanting for more. These fiscal traits will all affect your overall wants and needs when it comes to retirement and will likely affect the amount you need to retire comfortably. However, there are certain parts of your finances that everyone must consider.

The very first thing that you need to do when you establish your financial plan is to take a moment and really honestly determine what your circumstances are now in your life. Are you well to do? If you think you are, what does that mean?

- Determine your standard of living, current savings, and investments. You must be prepared to answer a number of questions to determine how you are living and your overall net worth:
    » How much do you and your spouse make in a year? Determine earnings that both you and your spouse make in a year from any source of income, such as salaries or consultant fees.
    » How much do you and your spouse typically spend? Are you and your spouse thrifty and frugal with your money or do you spend extravagantly? If you do spend most of your earned income, I would advise that you learn how to scale back as you approach retirement. However, you should always plan for the worst scenario and be honest about how much you really spend. Referencing things such as bank and credit card statements could be a good strategy. They will be more honest with you than you are

willing to be with yourself. Consult your statements to find the truth.
- » What are your assets? Things such IRAs, 401(k) s, non-qualified plans, stock portfolios, mutual funds, real estate investments, CDs, and insurance policies all give you a positive net worth. Find out where they all are and what their current worth is.
- » What are your concrete foreseeable expenses and liabilities? Factor in your expenses and liabilities that you know you will have to pay every year such as mortgages, car payments, and taxes. These will be constant drains on your wealth and will have to be factored into your overall value to see where you truly stand.
- After you have discovered where you stand, determine what your retirement goals will be. Do you want to tour the world for a year? Do you want to spend more time with family? Are you buying a new home? Will you be indulging any of your hobbies? Some habits like golfing or sailing can get quite expensive; make sure you factor these costs into your overall plan. Be honest about how much everything is going to cost. Give the dreams real value so that you can take real steps to achieving them.
- You will also want to find out what your annual living expenses are. The standard of living you have now and your goals for retirement are important to how you will spend in your retirement. The conventional wisdom is you need between 70% and 100% of your current salary annually in order to live a comfortable retirement.[1] Figure 4.1 demonstrates that many people believe that they will be able to maintain the same standard of living in retirement. However, when they reach retirement they realize how difficult it can be to maintain their lifestyle. What many people do not appreciate is the amount of planning it takes to have the same standard of living without having earned income.

THE RETIREMENT PITFALL

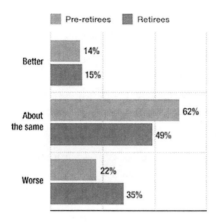

Source: NPR, Robert Wood Johnson Foundation, Harvard School of Public Health

Figure 4.1 – How Will You Live In Retirement Compared to Before Retirement? [2]

It is crucial that you back your beliefs with plans and information. First, determine what age it is that you and your spouse will retire. Having an age at which you plan to retire makes retirement planning much easier. This way you can determine how many years you will be out of work until you reach your life expectancy. This will assist in creating a more accurate financial model of what your retirement will look like. People often expect to retire in their late 60s. However, as Figure 4.2 demonstrates, most actually end up retiring in their 50s and early 60s. Many also live for longer than they expected. This early retirement age and extended retirement period could stretch your savings and possibly reduce your Social Security benefits. Try to stick to your planned retirement age to reduce your financial burden. As for your retirement period, make sure you add at least 5 to 10 years to your plan after your life expectancy to be safe. Fortunately for your nerves, but unfortunately for your finances, no one is sure when they will die. It's always better to have more savings than you need than to out-live them.

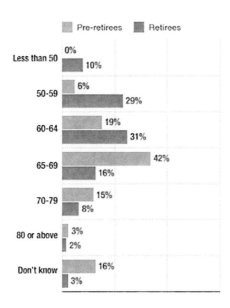

Figure 4.2 Pre-Retirees' Expected and Retirees' Realized Retirement Age[2]

Finding the amount of money you will need in retirement can be a difficult calculation. Your present age, life expectancy, Social Security benefits, along with all your investment choices will affect what you will need in retirement. If you would like to find this number by yourself there are plenty of financial calculators online. One can even be found on our website which is listed at the end of this book. Of course, a qualified financial advisor can help you determine your number as well.

Step 2: How Will You Get There?

After you determine the income you need now and the income that you will need in the future you must ascertain how you will get this money. Sometimes your savings and investments alone will not reach the number you desire, but there are many ways in which to

◄ THE RETIREMENT PITFALL

increase your income as you prepare for retirement. Many people simply think in terms of stocks and bonds and do not consider all of the options available to them when preparing their financial plans.

Most people do have some sort of solid or stable income that will pay continuously throughout their retirement. This will normally be the foundation of your retirement because it is unlikely that the money that you get from these sources will change considerably. Social Security was established as one of these sources. It is a way for society to provide relief for the elderly poor and is meant to be a reliable source of income. For many elderly, it is what they depend on to get by. Unfortunately, Social Security can be a convoluted process. The Social Security administration does guarantee your benefits once they have begun, but what they do not do is provide you assistance in managing the Social Security System. For your benefit in managing this system, Social Security will be discussed in depth in the Social Security chapter of this book.

Pensions from both private employers and government agencies are quickly becoming something of the past, but pensions are another item that many retirees depend on as a stable source of income. There are still many other sources to consider when thinking about your retirement income. What kind of retirement savings plan do you have? If you have a defined contribution plan there are a plethora of plans that you may have. The 401(k) plan is the most popular type of defined contribution plan but there are many others as well. The Cash Balance Plan, SIMPLE IRA, SEP IRA, Employee Stock Ownership Plan (ESOP), 457 Plan, and 403(b) Plan are all examples of defined contribution plans. All of which have their own unique sets of tax and legal intricacies. These intricacies can have tremendous effects on how you should withdraw your money from these accounts. You may withdraw from these defined contribution plans in a lump sum, in an income-type format, or roll them over into various assortments of retirement plans. Some of the plans are taxed, some are tax-deferred, and others are tax free. The method that you employ to withdraw your money can affect the staying power of your retirement plans. Make

FINANCIAL PLANNING FOR RETIREMENT

sure that you understand your options in order to make the correct choice for your future.

Another wealth increasing activity that you may want to consider in retirement is part-time work. Part-time work could fill the gap between your solid pension and Social Security income and the income that you have determined you need each year for your retirement; all while lightening the demands you are making on your investments. By taking part time work you can quit your primary career and therefore get access to your pension. You could also take part-time work in a presumably less demanding and more enjoyable job while still supplementing your income.

You may also expect to receive an inheritance in the near future, but I caution you again, do not count on or spend this money until you actually are in physical possession of it. What you can do in the mean time is make sure that when the money passes to you that you distribute it in the most efficient way possible. If you come into a large amount of money, you may put that sum into something that will continue to pay. As you age you will want to create income streams for yourself, so investments such as income producing investments may be something that could provide you with a safe and secure source of cash flow.

Additionally, real estate is a long term investment that may provide slow but steady income. There have been a few recent hiccups in the real estate market, but most investors are confident that the market has corrected itself. The real value in real estate is the continuous income that renters can provide. Renting your property will provide additional income for retirement. If you have property going into retirement, you will have to make the decision as to whether or not to sell the property for an immediate profit or to rent the property for income. Beware; renting real estate does involve work at times.

If you have a business it could also weigh heavily in getting what you want out of retirement. You have options as to how your business could contribute. Selling the business could give you a large lump sum that could be reinvested in other securities. These securi-

◄ THE RETIREMENT PITFALL

ties could provide more of the liquid assets and cash flow that you will need in retirement. On the other hand, you could keep the business and simply hand its operation over to someone that you trust. This could provide you with long-term continuous income that could increase if you leave the business in the right hands. Of course, this is a gamble. You always run the risk of your successor running the business into the ground, which could be disastrous for everyone involved, including yourself.

Step 3: Preparing For the Unknown

There are some things in this world that we have no way of avoiding. Sadly, disease and death are a fact of life and it is uncertain when they will occur. You also cannot stop a tornado from destroying your home, or prevent a flood from destroying your business. Likewise, there are things in government and politics that cannot be prevented by a single person. Individually we have little control when war strikes or when Uncle Sam comes knocking for tax. While these events in our life are largely unavoidable, that does not mean that you cannot prepare for them.

Let us begin with the most important thing in your life: your health. Science and medicine have made incredible improvements in the both the quality of living for human kind and the length of the average human life. However, with getting older comes a greater risk of having some kind of considerable health issue. People are living much longer these days and are surviving medical conditions that would have killed in the past. It is impossible to know if you or a loved one may be stricken with an illness that may cost a large amount of money. This means that the need for living assistance and long term care has increased. As you age, the possibility of you or your spouse having at least a brief stay at a long-term care facility will increase dramatically. As many as 6 out of 10 people will need long-term care services at least once during their lives.[3] Do you have the money to fund a long term care stay that could cost around an extra $6,000 monthly? How dramatically would this sudden increase in spend-

FINANCIAL PLANNING FOR RETIREMENT

ing affect your planned annual income? If your spouse is still living at home, long term care would only add to your monthly expenses. Make sure you have the financial tools available to deal with such a crisis and have the wealth to absorb this financial shock.

What about tax? Nearly every investment you make for retirement will have large tax implications for either now or down the road when you begin to withdraw from the account. Taxes are one of the most significant challenges you face to building significant wealth, and there is absolutely no guarantee that taxes will remain the way that they are today. In fact, it's almost a guarantee that the tax code will change at some point in our lives, either up or down. Considering the current financial crisis and the massive U.S. debt, its possible taxes could be increasing soon, especially since we are currently living in some of the lowest tax rates in U.S. history. Additionally, many people believe that you will be in a lower tax bracket when you retire because you will have a lower annual income, but this may not be true. Most people plan to have the same standard of living in retirement which means they will maintain the same levels of income, and therefore they will stay in the same tax bracket.

Take a look at Figure 4.3 below. When you retire, are you completely sure that your taxes will be lower considering the debt crisis in Washington? The possibility they won't be is certainly something to consider especially in light of historical data. Fortunately, there are investments such as Roth IRAs that can pay taxes on your investments now if you fear higher taxes later. If you use these tools correctly, then you will be able avoid taxes in retirement by avoiding moving into higher tax brackets. In order to qualify for the tax-free, penalty-free withdrawal of earnings, a Roth IRA must be in place for at least five tax years and the distribution must take place after age 59 ½.

THE RETIREMENT PITFALL

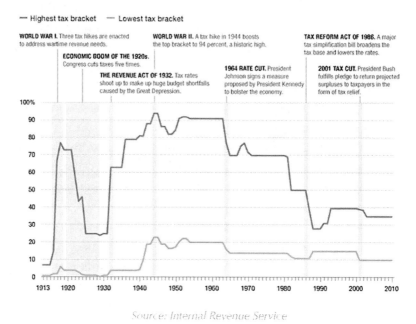

Figure 4.3 – Highs and Lows of Marginal Tax Rates[4]

You must also realize that when you retire, you will no longer be an income earner. This means that unless you take steps to prevent it, inflation will have a serious eroding effect on the purchasing power of your money. There is no way to predict rates of inflation far into the future, but in our economic system, inflation is almost a certainty. Remember what it used to cost to buy a candy bar at the local store? How much does that same candy cost now? Inflation is very real and accumulates much faster than one may think. What may seem like a safe retirement number when you begin retirement may look less and less appealing as time goes on because of the effects of inflation. Do the math and add at least a 3% annual inflation to expenses that will be affected. Expenses such as car payments and mortgages are fixed so you will not need to account for inflation for them. However, things like utilities, food, insurance, and travel will get more expensive as time goes on. Make sure you know what their costs will really look like in the future. A good hedge against inflation is to have money in investments that keep pace with inflation. Use these in order to keep your savings growing and healthy.

As we have found out recently, investment income is not guaranteed. Many people saw the market of the 1980s and 1990s and thought that the gains would never end. Many people began to throw caution to the wind and began to invest heavily in risky ventures in order to maximize returns. As 2007 rolled around they saw all of their investments fall to pieces and lost a considerable portion of their life savings in a relatively short period of time. When investing for retirement you must take into account that the stock market can be a dangerous place. You must realize that retirement is a long-term investment and you must build a portfolio that will not self destruct when the winds of change blow. Know exactly what it is you want your portfolio to do and design a portfolio that takes the least amount of risk to get there. Some less risky investments may get you to the same place that more risky investments do. Make sure your portfolio is as efficient as possible to avoid a disaster.

Find out what investment products work best for your circumstances. Then you will be able to find the most direct path to the goal you set for yourself. If you would like to try to design your investments yourself, help is available. There are plenty of Monte Carlo calculators that will take your investments and subject them to random market occurrences to test how those investments may work for you. It is always better to be over prepared than under prepared.

When talking about retirement you must also be prepared to talk about death and the impact it will have on your family. This is especially true of your spouse if he/she survives you. It is always tragic when a spouse dies. It is especially tragic when they have not properly planned for their demise. This is because the surviving spouse may then have a severely limited income after their partner's death, but they still have exactly the same amount of bills. It may be hard to think about your own death, let alone plan for it, but you owe it to your loved ones to make it so they are able to live comfortably after you pass. Determine what would change for your loved ones if you

◄ THE RETIREMENT PITFALL

were to die suddenly. Properly planning your estate can also have a dramatic effect on how well your estate is managed after you have died.

Step 4: Stay Flexible

For some planning is a cinch. What is more difficult for these individuals is changing their "perfect" plan after it has leapt from their intensely powerful mind. However, very often in order to have a functioning, real-world plan this is what you must do. There is a quotation from General Dwight D. Eisenhower that sums up this essential aspect of planning:

"In preparing for battle, I have always found that plans are useless but planning is indispensable."

Though General Eisenhower was referring to his experiences as a battlefield commander in the above quotation, the message of his quotation is applicable to life as a whole. A plan itself is good only at the moment. If you build a plan that is stagnant, you are building a plan that will eventually become obsolete. It is great to have a plan, it is even better to have a flexible plan, but the plan of all plans must be actively, consistently, revamped to meet changes.

Imagine your retirement plan like the engine of a car. Would you simply construct an engine and expect it to run forever? Of course not! Even the best engines need oil changes, tune ups, and parts repaired in order to keep it running. Your retirement plan needs work as well to keep it in running shape. It is excellent to make a plan, but make sure you make time to adjust it according to new happenings.

Unfortunately, life does not always turn out the way we would like it to. Therefore, we must discuss what you can do even when the world is working against you. When change does occur, it is best to change your plan in a way that does not interfere with your overall objective. You should not compromise on your goals, because if you do end up compromising on the end game, you are essentially giving up on your wants. Do not do this unless you absolutely have to.

Often, the first things that retirees will do in response to a setback are panic and change their investments. Many people will take this course of action because it seems easier than the other ways to fix your plan. This should be your final option in trying to repair a retirement plan. Changing your investments may seem easy, but there can be severe consequences to such a decision. If you have lost money in investments or suddenly lost a job, you run the risk of making things worse by attempting to recoup your losses in investments with bigger returns. Bigger returns mean bigger risk, and potentially bigger loss. If you lose out on that gamble, then you're really in a pickle. Anything really worth having takes work.

There are safer things that you can change to maintain your goals:
- Change the level of income you are presently receiving. If you cut your retirement income and reduce your expenses now in order to extend the life of your investments, it may be possible to reach your goals despite significant setbacks.
- Change the time frame in which you would be receiving benefits. If you push your retirement up from 62 to 65, that could significantly change the amount of money needed for retirement because you will work for three more years. Those were three years that you actually expected to receive income instead of making it. That's a big change for your bottom line.
- Increase your contribution to your retirement plan. If you increase your contributions, your investments will have the potential to grow larger, and you could have more income accessible when you decide to withdraw your money. During retirement you could also take a part time job to help supplement your income. Choose something you enjoy and it will hardly seem like work at all.

Be Investment Smart

To a novice investor, the market can indeed be an intimidating place. There are so many products and rules regarding the investment industry that it can often just not make sense. Here is some advice that will make it easier to manage planning your finances.

◄ **THE RETIREMENT PITFALL**

- Be Sure You Are Understanding Statistics Correctly - Sometimes statistics will look appealing from the outside, but in reality they are not what they seem. For instance, many stocks and funds will list their annual gains and losses right next to each other. If a stock is valued at $100, loses 33% of its value in year one, and then makes a gain of 33% in year two, what is the value of the stock? If you answered $100 then you are wrong, but have made a common mistake that many investors do not notice. When the stock takes a loss of 33% in the first year, the value of that stock will drop to $67. The following year an increase of 33% will not bring the stock's value up to $100 again. That 33% increase is now based on the new stock value of $67. A 33% increase of $67 will result in a new value of roughly $89. So despite having a loss and then a gain of the same percentile value, your stock is now actually worth less. Be very wary of statistical tricks such as this one when investing. Average returns are not actual returns. Losing money in the beginning of an investment will not be that noticeable in your annual returns, but will change what your returns look like later on in your investment.
- Asset Allocation – Letting your assets grow is excellent, but every now and then you must make corrections to your investment. Your portfolio should be like a garden. The plants should be allowed to grow, but you must also prune and weed for it to stay healthy. Set up an overall design of your stock, bond, and money market ratios. If your investments grow so that your ratio becomes distorted, it is important that you correct it to maintain your same level of risk. Plans that grow unattended mutate into things they were not intended to be. If you would like more information on asset management please look into our later chapters.
- Be Careful With Your Retirement Savings – Don't make the egregious mistake of taking money out of your retirement plans before you retire. You are then going in reverse. You lose

overall principle in your account and therefore lose any interest or gains you may have been able to lay claim to. Not only that, you could also encounter some withdrawal penalties. Withdrawing from a retirement plan before retirement should be an absolute last resort. Also, be careful when moving your retirement savings. If you do need to move your money, make sure that you do it in the most tax efficient way possible.

When designing a retirement plan, it is important to have a procedure to follow in order to reach your objectives. The considerations presented in this chapter are numerous, but thinking about them before taking action is as important as making the moves themselves. There is no magic formula for having a successful retirement. This chapter is simply a guide. Hard work and sound guidance can help you reach a happy retirement, but being prepared and adapting your plans are the only ways to keep your retirement engine running.

Chapter 5 Endnotes

1. "How Much Retirement Income Do You Need?" *CBSNews*. CBS Interactive, 21 Apr. 2010. Web. 07 May 2012. <http://www.cbsnews.com/8301-505146_162-39940707/how-much-retirement-income-do-you-need/>.
2. Rovner, Julie. "Boomers' 'Delusion' About Health In Retirement." *NPR*. NPR, 28 Sept. 2011. Web. 08 May 2012. <http://www.npr.org/2011/09/28/140853479/boomers-delusion-about-health-in-retirement?ps=rs>.
3. "How to Prepare for Your Long-Term Care Needs." - *The Best Life (usnews.com)*. Web. 06 Apr. 2012. <http://money.usnews.com/money/blogs/the-best-life/2011/11/01/how-to-prepare-for-your-long-term-care-needs-2>.
4. Zarroli, Jim, and NPR Staff. "Would The Buffett Rule Help The U.S. Economy?" *NPR*. NPR, 11 Apr. 2012. Web. 11 Apr. 2012. <http://www.npr.org/2012/04/11/150406660/what-would-the-buffett-rule-mean-for-the-u-s-economy>.

CHAPTER 6

Social Security

"Social Security... reflects some of our deepest values—the duties we owe to our parents, the duties we owe to each other when we're differently situated in life, the duties we owe to our children and our grandchildren. Indeed, it reflects our determination to move forward across generations and across the income divides in our country, as one America."
– William J. Clinton

FOR DECADES, SOCIAL Security has been one of the most important parts of retirement for many seniors. Nearly every worker qualifies for it and it has shaped the look of retirement in America. Social Security is something that many people count on when they are in need and is something they expect when they are older. However, people know very little about the Social Security System because of some of its puzzling rules. Knowing the system could be a serious advantage for the investment plans of a retiree, especially if the knowledge is used to make the payments from the system as efficient as possible. This chapter is dedicated to understanding the Social Security System and establishing a plan of action that will make the most of Social Security for us.

SOCIAL SECURITY

The Basics

The Great Depression left many Americans completely without hope. Millions were left without work and the deflation of the U.S. dollar made it almost impossible for a business to turn a profit. The result was throngs of destitute Americans looking for relief. Those that were especially vulnerable to this crisis were the young and the old. While someone of working age could move on to find a job; someone that was older and retired who lost their sources of support had no choice but to suffer in poverty. In 1935, Franklin Delano Roosevelt put forward the Social Security Administration to relieve poverty in America. The official name of Social Security is the Old-Age Survivors and Disability Insurance program (OASDI) and was created to prevent the elderly from falling victim to the Great Depression. In the 2012 year, Social Security is funded through a payroll tax of 4.2% for employees and 6.2% for employers on the first $110,100 that every worker in America makes.

Though controversial when it was first introduced to Congress, it passed as part of FDRs "New Deal" and became a part of American life. In the 1960s, as part of Lyndon B. Johnson's "Great Society" program, Social Security took on Medicaid and Medicare, two new aspects that broadened its scope of services considerably. In the 1970s Social Security experienced yet another change when the federal government instituted COLAs or Cost Of Living Adjustments. This allowed the recipients of Social Security to receive increases in their Social Security payments based on CPI (Consumer Price Index) increases. These COLAs are announced every year and increase the benefits of all Social Security Beneficiaries by the announced percentage. The results of the additions of Medicaid, Medicare, and COLAs have made the Social Security Administration a mammoth agency. It takes up more of the U.S. budget than any other federal program. In fact, Social Security has become, and likely will continue to be, the largest government program in the world.

◄ THE RETIREMENT PITFALL

The Math

Millions of Americans depend on the social security program. It keeps millions of elderly from slipping below the federal poverty line and also provides assistance to the most vulnerable in our society; namely the young, the old, and the disabled. Each quarter of the year that you work a Social Security covered job, you receive a credit. You must earn $1,090 in a quarter to earn a credit and you may earn 4 credits a year. An individual becomes fully insured by Social Security when they work 40 quarters or 10 years in a Social Security covered job.

The thing that separates Social Security from most of the rest of your retirement income is its dependability. The amount of money that you will be getting from the system is based on a formula that takes into account your earnings while you were working. Therefore, the amount that you will eventually receive from the Social Security System is easy to predict. The way that the government predicts your Social Security income is they take the average of the highest 35 years of earnings you have made in your lifetime. If you worked less than 35 years, the remaining years you did not work will have zeros put in their place. Add these 35 years of earnings up and divide this total by 420 (the amount of months in 35 years) and you will have your Average Indexed Monthly Earnings or AIME. This AIME is then put through a three part formula that calculates your insurance coverage under social security or the Premium Insurance Amount (PIA). The first $767 of your AIME is multiplied by 90%, the amount between $767 and $4624 ($3857) is multiplied by 32% and any amount over $4624 is multiplied by 15%. Add these three products up and you have your Primary Insurance Amount (PIA).

Let's try and put this into practice. Assume that Mr. Smith is ready to retire with a nice and neat AIME of $10,000. The first $767 would be multiplied by 90% for a total of $690, the second $3857 (between $767 and $4624) would be multiplied by 32% for $1234, and the final $5376 (of 10,000) would be multiplied by 15% for $806. Add these three numbers up and you have Mr. Smith's PIA of $2731. This will be Mr. Smith's monthly benefit for the rest of his life; not taking

SOCIAL SECURITY

into account COLA increases, and assuming he began taking Social Security payments at 66 years old.

If you were born between 1943 and 1954, sixty-six is the age at which you are fully eligible for your Social Security benefits, but you may begin claiming early benefits at age 62. However, there is a catch. If you do decide to claim early retirement benefits, you will receive a reduced benefit. If you apply for benefits between the age of 62 and 65 your benefits will be reduced to 75% of your calculated PIA. In the case of Mr. Smith that means that instead of receiving his full PIA of $2731 per month, he would only get $2048. The worst part about claiming early eligibility is that the early eligibility amount is permanent. You may never claim your full PIA. The only way that your benefits could increase is through annual COLAs. This could have a tremendous impact on the amount of Social Security you receive throughout your life. For some people that earn a low income or are forced into retirement, your financial situation will require that you take benefits sooner rather than later. If that is the case, early eligibility may be necessary. However, if at all possible, attempt to wait until your full benefit age at 66 to claim your Social Security benefits. The impact on your retirement finances could be significant.

What if the opposite is true? What if you are still working and do not necessarily need the additional income at age 66 when you reach full eligibility? This is where it can get interesting. At 66 you have technically reached full eligibility, but for every year that you do not claim your social security benefits, you gain what is called a delayed credit. A delayed credit will increase your Social Security benefit by 8% for every year you do not claim eligibility until age 70. This means that Mr. Smith's PIA of $2731 per month would increase by 8% every year until 70, leaving him with a maximum possible benefit of $3605. The higher benefit may seem great, but the problem is that none of us know when we are going to die. Because of this, if you forgo the income at age 66 for the higher paycheck at 70 and then die young, you have lost a large amount of possible Social Security income. There are ways to determine when the larger income starting at age 70 will

THE RETIREMENT PITFALL

surpass the more spread income beginning at age 66, you just have to make your best guess as to whether you will live that long. Determine your "breakeven point" and to determine what age it would be best for you to claim benefits. It may be difficult, but you must be honest with yourself and others about your health and well-being to determine your appropriate age to begin making withdrawals.

Delayed credits can be a positive and it may be beneficial for people to wait to take their Social Security at age 70. The point at which the value of your delayed benefits will surpass the value of your normal benefits is normally somewhere in your mid-seventies. These days, most people live beyond 75 or 76, so delaying your benefits has a good chance of paying off. Additionally, it helps to think of your Social Security benefits and the delayed credits as an investment. What other investment is going to guarantee you 8% return every year for four years and then pay you that top dollar amount every month for the rest of your life? Deals like that just don't exist. If you are able and it makes sense for your situation, consider taking advantage of the offer being given to you by the U.S. government.

Age of Application	Benefit will be % of PIA	If PIA is $2,731
62	75.0%	$2,048
63	80.0%	$2,185
64	86.7%	$2,368
65	93.3%	$2,548
66	100%	$2,731
67	108%	$2,949
68	116%	$3,168
69	124%	$3,386
70	132%	$3,605

Figure 5.1 – How Age Changes Benefits

Even if you do not start taking benefits, once you reach age 62 COLAs will increase your eventual benefit from the Social Security

SOCIAL SECURITY

Administration. For instance, if Mr. Smith begins taking benefits when he is 66 and there was COLA increases in the years since he was 62, those COLAs will be added to his PIA even though he was not talking benefits at that time. The problem with COLAs is that there is no way to determine if there will be a COLA increase year to year, so it isn't exactly something that you can depend on. Most experts use an annual increase of 2.8% to estimate Social Security increases, but this is no guarantee.

Love and Marriage

Social Security does take into account whether you are married or not. Depending on your marital status, your overall benefits will change. If you had been married or are married at the time you begin collecting Social Security you may apply for spousal benefits. If your spouse did not work and therefore did not establish any Social Security benefits for her or himself, he or she still may collect spousal benefits. Social Security allows your spouse to collect half of what the primary earner receives. Since Mr. Smith has a PIA of $2731, Mrs. Smith would then be able to collect $1366 under his PIA calculations. If a spouse did work, but has earned a PIA that is considerably less than the other spouse's PIA, the first spouse's lower PIA can be compensated up to 50% of the other spouse's larger PIA. For instance, if Mrs. Smith did work and earned a $500 PIA, she would still be allowed to collect $1366 in accordance with her husband's earnings. Also, a spouse's benefit will not increase based on an increase in the benefits of the other spouse. For example, if Mr. Smith waited until 70 to receive his benefits and earned delayed credits, Mrs. Smith's spousal benefits would not increase. She would still only receive her original $1366 spousal benefit.

If you are widowed, Social Security will offer you something called survivor benefits. Survivor benefits are different than your spousal benefits in that you will receive 100% of the benefit that your spouse was receiving in the event he or she dies. You are also entitled to a one time lump sum payment of $255 upon the death of your

◂ THE RETIREMENT PITFALL

spouse. You may apply for survivor benefits at age 60. However, much like normal Social Security benefits, your benefits will be reduced if you apply before age 66. If you are earning your own benefit, then it may not make sense to take a survivor benefit at all. You are permitted to take your own Social Security benefit or your survivor benefit; whichever one is greater, but you may not take both. In the case of the Smiths, it would definitely be in Mrs. Smith's interest to take her husband's survivor benefit of $2731 over her own $500 benefit.

Important notes about survivor benefits: Survivor benefits are different than spousal benefits in that they are affected by delaying your initial Social Security benefits. If Mr. Smith waited until he was 70 to begin taking payments, when he died Mrs. Smith would receive the same amount her husband was receiving with the delayed benefits. In other words, she would get his actual benefit, not the initial PIA calculation. If you are concerned about how your spouse will afford things if you were to suddenly pass, it may be in your interest to delay benefits to provide that extra assistance if it is needed. The Social Security office will never pay two benefits to one person at the same time. If you choose to take your deceased spouse's survivor benefit, your personal benefits will stop. Also, if you remarry you will lose your survivor benefits, unless you remarry after age 60.

If you divorce there are a whole different set of rules for you. Divorced couples still may have claim to their ex-spouse's Social Security benefits. If you were married for 10 years, divorced, and did not remarry; you still may claim spousal benefits. You do not need to wait for your ex-spouse to claim benefits in order to take spousal benefits for yourself either, as long as you have been divorced for 2 years. All that is needed is proof that you two were indeed married. The ex-spouse may also collect full survivor benefits when the other spouse dies. So watch out because you may be worth more dead!

Work and Income

- *Before Retirement Age*: If you work while receiving Social Security Benefits this may limit the amount of benefits you are able to receive. When you do work, your earnings will be subjected to the earnings test. The amount that you are able to make without losing Social Security income changes with the rate of inflation, but in 2012 the amount is presently $14,640 if you have not yet reached full retirement age or NRA (Normal Retirement Age).[2] This number essentially means that if you are claiming early eligibility for Social Security, your first $14,640 in earnings will not affect the amount of Social Security benefits you receive. However, if your earnings exceed this amount then for every $2 that you make over the limit $1 will be withheld from your benefits. These lost benefits will be added back to your total when your benefits are recalculated at full retirement age, but the 25% reduction for early eligibility will still apply.

- *The Year You Reach Full Retirement Age*: The year in which you reach retirement age changes the earnings test. The entire year will not count toward your earnings, only the months before the month of your birthday, and in 2012 the limit that you may earn without causing a withholding of your benefits has been raised to $38,880. So if Mr. Smith was to turn 66 in May, only his earnings from January to April would count toward the withholding limit. If you make more than $38,880 before your birth month in the year you turn 66, then for every $3 that you make that year, $1 will be withheld from your benefits above that amount. Also, earnings made that year before you apply for benefits do not count against you. So if Mr. Smith applied for benefits in April of 2012 and made $100,000 before April, this would not affect the level of benefits he would receive. Mr. Smith would be subject to a monthly limit which is calculated by splitting the yearly cap into 12 month chunks. For example, in the year Mr. Smith reaches full retirement age his monthly earnings limit is $3240 ($38,880 divided by 12).

If you do exceed the income limits, Social Security will normally withhold part of your Social Security benefits ahead

THE RETIREMENT PITFALL

of time, but only if you let them know exceeding the earnings limits is a possibility. For instance, if you make $20,000 when you are claiming benefits at 62 then you are $5360 dollars over the limit and Social Security will withhold $2680 of your benefits that year.

If you do not let them know, then you may face paying back your withheld benefits at the end of the year. Just like with income tax, the objective should be to not owe Social Security any money at the end of the year. With that in mind, try and be as accurate as possible about your annual income so that your benefits are withheld at the beginning of the year instead of demanded all at the end.

- *After You Reach Full Retirement Age*: When you reach full retirement age you then have the ability to work and earn as much as you want without penalty on your Social Security benefits. Be careful though, your benefits will not be affected, but the more you earn the more your Social Security will be taxed. Read on to learn more about tax and your Social Security benefits.

Retirement plans such as 401(k) s and IRAs will not affect your ability to collect Social Security. You may take as much and as many retirement plan distributions as you want without affecting the level of benefits you are receiving. However, the amount of income you receive through these conduits will affect the level of tax on your Social Security benefits, so beware.

Tax

After you begin to receive your Social Security benefits, there is not much that will change the actual amount of money you are receiving, but given certain situations, the government will most definitely try to tax it back. Your benefits are taxed depending on your income. Not earned income; but a mysterious amount called provisional income that takes into account things such as withdrawals from investments. This is where it becomes important to assess how

SOCIAL SECURITY

much money you are taking in distributions from things such as IRAs and 401(k)s. As you can see in Figure 5.2 below, if you are single and making over $25,000 in a year, your Social Security benefits will jump from tax free to 50% of your benefits being taxed. If you exceed $34,000 in income as an individual, 85% of your income will be taxable. If you are married and filing jointly the thresholds for the tax rates are slightly higher, but the rate of tax on your benefits will be the same once you exceed the limits. These tax levels are fixed and are not increased through the CPI or any other device. This means that as inflation increases, it becomes less and less possible to avoid being taxed on your social security income while maintaining a reasonable standard of living. There is really no way to avoid this tax short of not passing these thresholds. This is the government's sneaky way to make sure that Social Security goes to those who need it. If you have money, they want their money back.

	Income	Percentage of Social Security Taxable
Single, Head of Household, Qualifying Widower and Married Filing Separately (where the spouses lived apart the entire year)	Below $25,000	All SS income is tax-free
	$25,000 - $34,000	Up to 50% of SS income may be taxable
	$34,000 and up	Up to 85% of SS may be taxable
Married Filing Jointly	Below $32,000	All SS income is tax-free
	$32,000 - $44,000	Up to 50% of SS income may be taxable
	$44,000 and up	Up to 85% of SS may be taxable

Figure 5.2 – Taxable Social Security Income[3]

The only thing that can be done to avoid tax on your Social Security benefits is to prepare for it. You may want to wait until 70 to take bigger benefits. These larger benefits will raise your over-me without triggering Social Security taxes. You could then structure your payments from your retirement plans so that you won't break theses ceilings and subject yourself to unnecessary tax. This way when you do begin taking Social Security, you are able to avoid as much taxation as possible while still enjoying income. Of course, if you are on the verge of breaking one of these tax thresholds and you are working, you could always work less to avoid raising your taxes. It may be a better financial option to work less and avoid triggering Social Security tax rather than breaking the tax threshold and losing more money in tax than you earned in income from that extra work.

It would be beneficial to know what your provisional income is because provisional income is the figure the government uses to tax your Social Security payments. Once your provisional income is known, it is then possible to avoid tax increases by doing things that do not increase your provisional income amount. Things such as investment income must be declared in provisional income so one of the ways to lower your overall provisional income is by reducing your income declared on investments. One way that you may be able to lower your investment income while using Social Security is using your IRA before you apply for Social Security. For example, if you are 62, it may be better to put off applying for Social Security and use your IRA to live until you are 66. This way you are able to avoid tax by using investment income before you start your Social Security benefits, thereby using what would be provisional income before it becomes a tax issue. This strategy would also avoid having to use early eligibility benefits by allowing you to reach full retirement age.

If you still have a large amount of money in retirement plans and are ready to start Social Security, there is another useful way to avoid tax. By converting your IRAs into Roth IRA accounts, you eliminate that money as taxable income. You are then able to withdraw from those Roth accounts freely while collecting tax free Social Security benefits. Just be sure to have enough money saved to cover the taxes on the Roth conversion if you implement this strategy.

Changing Your Benefits

For the most part, when you apply for eligibility in the Social Security System the payment you receive will not change for life; other than the occasional COLA increase. However, in certain circumstances there may be ways to actually change the benefits you are receiving.

- The passage of the Seniors Citizens Right to Work Act of 2000 allows for a "File and Suspend" of Social Security benefits. Let us assume there is a higher earning husband and there is a lower earning wife. When the higher earning spouse reaches full retirement age, he may file for benefits and then "file and suspend". This then allows the lower earning spouse to apply for spousal benefits under her partner's name while the higher earning spouse's benefits are suspended. When he stops his payments, he begins accruing delayed credits again. The "file and suspend" will not change rates for the lesser earning spouse, but that is not the objective of this maneuver. The real advantage is having a lesser earning spouse receive benefits while the higher earning spouse "suspends" and still collects delayed credits until age 70 and, thus, gets a higher monthly payment. Please note, if your spouse is younger than 66 when she applies for a spousal benefit she will be subject to a reduced benefit. Reduced benefits are based on your individual ages, regardless of the age of the person filing. For instance, if Mrs. Smith files for spousal benefits at age 62 she will she receive a reduced benefit, even though Mr. Smith has reached full retirement age at 66.
- If an individual begins taking benefits before their wealthier spouse applied for Social Security, they may eventually be able to take a larger spousal benefit. If the amount that she receives is less than she would get if she began taking her husband's spousal benefits, she could take the higher spousal benefit when her husband begins taking Social Security benefits. This is allowed because you may not use a spousal

◄ THE RETIREMENT PITFALL

benefit from someone who is not yet taking Social Security payments themselves. Once a person begins taking benefits, the new applicant's spouse may hop on their plan and take their spousal benefit if they choose. However, if the spouse began by taking a reduced benefit at age 62, that reduction would still apply to the spousal benefits. She would receive less than the full 50% benefit that you would receive if you apply for spousal benefits at full retirement age.

- Another way to change your payments is if you have reached your full retirement age, and are eligible for a spouse's or ex-spouse's benefit and your own retirement benefit, you may choose to receive only spousal benefits. If an individual is at full retirement age and married, he or she can file for a spousal benefit and delay filing for his or her own retirement benefit until a later time. If you do this, you can take advantage of delayed retirement credits and get a higher monthly benefit on your personal Social Security benefit later.[4]
- We all make mistakes; this applies to Social Security as well. Especially in an economy such as the one we live in today, the unexpected happens and while it may have seemed wise to apply for Social Security at one point, you may realize shortly thereafter that you have made a mistake. The good news is that there is a provision that allows you correct your mistake; the bad news is that this mistake must be corrected quickly. If you do decide to stop your Social Security benefits, you must withdraw your application within 12 months of becoming eligible for benefits.[5] After 12 months your benefits are permanent and cannot be reneged.

If you choose to withdraw your application don't expect the government to simply stop making payments. At this point you have taken money from the government. Money that you are no longer entitled to, and the government expects you to pay them back. Every dollar of your benefits must go back to the government in order for you to be able to reapply in the future. This includes repaying any spousal benefits or benefits to any other person under your application. If this is month 11 of receiving benefits, this check could be a considerable amount. In addition, every person that is receiving benefits under your application must give written consent for you to withdraw your application. This could prove challenging if they are depending on the money to make ends meet.

The moral of the story is when you apply, make sure that you are absolutely prepared for Social Security. If you must withdraw your application for Social Security, make sure you are prepared for the repercussions of such actions.

Social Security is an excellent government program, just be sure you take the time to use it in the best way possible. One of the best things about Social Security is, once you are qualified for Social Security, it cannot be taken away and the amount you receive will be increased according to any COLAs that the government makes. This makes the earnings from Social Security the basis on which many retirees design their retirement plans. When you begin taking Social Security benefits it is unlikely that there will be significant changes in the amount you receive even if the federal government begins to reform the system. Most changes will likely be to how people contribute to and how people come into the Social Security system, not to existing beneficiaries. Therefore, existing and soon-to-be beneficiaries need not worry about their Social Security benefits once they begin.

Medicare

Since Medicare is technically part of Social Security, we should take a minute to address it and see what can be done to fit it into your retirement plan. Surprisingly, most Baby Boomers need to be educated in the ways of Social Security. A study by the Bankers Life and Casualty Company's Center for a Secure Retirement, found that 56% of respondents admitted to knowing little or almost nothing about the Medicare program, 13% of respondents even falsely believed

◄ THE RETIREMENT PITFALL

Medicare is free. Indeed, 72% of Boomers did not know that most Americans on Medicare pay a monthly premium, co-pays and deductibles.[6] Chances are that Medicare will be a significant concern at some point during your retirement. Therefore, it is important to know the basics of the Medicare system. However, just like retirement in general, the Medicare plans that you need will be based specifically on your health care needs. There is no plan that fits every person, you must do your research.

1. Medicare Part A – Medicare Part A is the basic plan for all workers that pay basic Medicare premiums out of their paychecks throughout their life. Part A insurance helps cover inpatient care during hospital stays up to 90 days, inpatient care in a skilled nursing facility, home health care after a hospital stay, and hospice care. Keep in mind, when you are in the hospital, Medicare Part A will not cover the entire hospital stay. There are other deductibles and per diem expenses that need to be accounted for. Medicare Part A does not cover things like doctors and surgeons, or custodial, non-skilled, or long-term care activities; including help needed for activities of daily living (ADL) such as personal hygiene, cooking, and cleaning. As you can see, Part A covers your most basic medical costs but leaves out large areas of necessary modern medical coverage. You will need additional coverage to have a comprehensive insurance plan that will address your needs as you age. The majority of people will stay at some sort of long term care facility at some point in their life. It is especially important for most to have this Medicare gap filled by long term care insurance because these facilities can be quite expensive.

2. Medicare Part B – Medicare Part B is an optional coverage that most seniors elect to take in addition to Medicare Part A. This is because Medicare Part B covers many of the crucial gaps that Medicare Part A does not cover. The difference between Part A and Part B is that Part B requires a premium to

SOCIAL SECURITY

be paid for coverage, where as Part A does not. Medicare Part B acts similar to major medical policy and will cover about 80% of medical expenses after a small initial deductible. Part B covers doctor and surgeon services, home health services even if you were not in the hospital, lab tests and medical equipment, and doctor office visits. When someone qualifies for Part A, you may enroll for Part B three months before your Part A coverage begins. This enrollment period will last for 7 months after it begins. If you miss this enrollment date, you must enroll during Part B open enrollment which is January to March every year. It is crucial that you seriously consider enrolling in Part B coverage. Part B is often used far more than Part A and is more likely to assist you detecting any health problems before they become serious enough to need Part A coverage. Part B covers doctors and office visits. Part A covers long hospital stays. If you think about it, you'll need Part B even when you are using Part A. Will you simply sit in a hospital bed at the hospital? No. Doctors will come see you (and bill you), they will run tests and they may perform procedures and surgeries, all of which need Part B coverage. Protect your retirement funds from unexpected medical issues by having the proper Medicare coverage.

3. <u>Medicare Part C</u> – Also known as Medicare Advantage, Part C is actually run by private insurances. A Medicare Advantage Plan takes the place of Medicare Part A and Part B and will cover everything that Part A and Part B provide, however they may cover different amounts of those Part A and Part B items. This means that though a Part C plan must cover a hospital stay, they may not cover the stay as well as a traditional Part A plan would. Be cautious when shopping for a Part C plan and make sure that the coverage is what you need. On the plus side, Part C plans normally include some additional coverage such as hearing, dental, prescription and vision which may eliminate the need for other sources of insurance. You

may only be part of a single Part C plan at any time. Each Part C plan has different out of pocket costs and different ways that you receive services. This would be similar to common healthcare plans in that some require you to get a referral to see a specialist or you may only see certain doctors and institutions that are "in network" in non-emergency situations. You must choose according to your personal medical needs to have a plan that will best protect you. It is possible that a good Medicare C plan may eliminate the need for Medicare supplement insurance, but that will depend on your needs and preferences.

4. Medicare Part D – Part D coverage is Medicare's prescription drug plan. It is run by private companies and offers various options for the payment of premiums to cover necessary medications. If there are no private plans available in your area there is a standard plan. Part D's standard plan does have a deductible and also has a "donut hole" in the plan where $4,450 dollars of costs will go uncovered past about $3,000 in annual prescription expenses. If you do have a large number of prescriptions it is important that you get this donut hole in coverage filled with a supplemental insurance to avoid bleeding yourself dry on unnecessary drug costs.

5. Medicare Supplemental Insurance – Medicare Supplemental Plans are sold by private insurers and range from plans A through L. They are designed to cover the gaps in coverage that Medicare Plans A through D leave in coverage. All of these plans are different and cover specific needs. One of the most attractive features of supplemental plans is that many cover deductibles and cost sharing that is required in other Medicare plans, which could make most of your medical issues completely covered. Make sure that you review these plans and select one that best covers your medical concerns to save you money.

Medical insurance is of crucial importance during retirement, especially when you reach your advanced years. It is important to have comprehensive coverage, but also consider what it is you actually need. Buying a plan that will cover almost any medical concern is comforting, but will burn a deep hole in your pocket through insurance premiums. If The Affordable Care Act is deemed constitutional, it may make parts of Medicare such as prescriptions and preventative care more affordable for some people, but that remains to be seen. For now, we must operate under the assumption that the Medicare system will remain the same. Choose the plan that is most appropriate for you considering your medical health and family history. It is also valuable to consult a medical professional to determine when to enroll in these plans and what plan best suits your needs.

The U.S. Government has in place many programs designed to help the American public throughout their lives, but this is especially true in retirement. The poor and disabled are beneficiaries of Social Security, but at its core the program is to aid people in their retirement years. Medicare and Social Security will assist anyone that has paid their dues to the system, but it will most benefit those who have done their due diligence in understanding its inner workings. Once you know how it works, it then becomes easier to see how it could be used to assist you in your specific retirement situation. The government will not hold your hand while you are making decisions regarding Social Security. You getting the most out of the system actually means more revenue that must be spent on you, so I wouldn't expect guidance anytime soon. However, this money is revenue that you are entitled to after giving to the system throughout your working career. Take the time to make the right decisions for yourself and Social Security can be a steadfast ally during your retirement.

Chapter 6 Endnotes

1. 1. "Social Security." *Publications*. Web. 16 Apr. 2012 <http://www.ssa.gov/pubs/10070.html>.
2. "Exempt Amounts Under the Earnings Test." *The United States Social Security Administration*. Web. 17 Apr. 2012. <http://www.

ssa.gov/oact/COLA/rtea.html>.
3. "Avoid The Social Security Tax Trap." *Investopedia*. Web. 17 Apr. 2012. http://www.investopedia.com/articles/pf/08/social-security-tax.asp
4. "Other Things to Consider." *Retirement Planner:*. Web. 18 Apr. 2012. <http://www.socialsecurity.gov/retire2/otherthings.htm>.
5. "If You Change Your Mind." *Retirement Planner:*. Web. 18 Apr. 2012. <http://www.ssa.gov/retire2/withdrawal.htm>.
6. "Financial Planning." *Bankers Life Study Finds That Middle-income Americans Know Little about Medicare*. Web. 20 Apr. 2012. <http://www.financial-planning.com/news/Bankers-Life-Secure-Retirement-Medicare-Study-Financial-Planning-2677575-1.html?zkPrintable=true>.

CHAPTER 7

Retirement Plans/IRAs

"Let our advance worrying become advance thinking and advance planning"
  – Winston Churchill

SINCE THE DECLINE of the defined benefit plans in the 1960s and the rise of the defined contribution plans in the 1970s the world of retirement planning has become more complicated for the individual retiree. The days of consistent, dependable income coming from your employer are extremely rare. Today it is expected that you are responsible for your own savings and investments for your later years. However, with more responsibility comes more opportunity. The fact that you are able to design the plan that works best for you enables you to surpass the retirement expectations of someone in a similar situation under a defined benefit plan. The trick is knowing how to use the plans available to you as effectively as possible.

First let's cover the general information. The retirement plan that people come across first in their lives is normally the employer sponsored retirement plans. According to federal law, a qualified retirement plan must be in compliance with the Employee Retirement Income Security Act of 1974 (ERISA). Among the most commonly used qualified retirement plans are: The 401(k) Plan, Solo 401(k), Simplified Employee Pension Plan (SEP), Savings Incentive Match

◄ THE RETIREMENT PITFALL

Plan for Employees (SIMPLE), 457 Plan, and 403(b) Plan. All are effective ways to meet particular retirement planning needs, but by far the 401(k) plan is the most popular employer sponsored qualified plan. Because the 401(k) plan is so widely and commonly used, it is important that we talk about the specifics of that ubiquitous plan, but first let's briefly cover the aspects of other possible retirement plans.

- Traditional IRA – A traditional IRA is a personal retirement account that allows an investor to use pre-tax income to fund their investments, which then grows on a tax deferred basis. The principle and gains are finally taxed when they are withdrawn from the account. An individual may give 100% of their earned income to their IRA in 2012 up to $5,000; or $6,000 if you are over 50.
- SEP IRA – These plans are designed to allow small business owners an easy way to provide retirement benefits to their employees. Costs on the plan are low because the formula for the plan is simple. All participants in a SEP IRA are to receive the same amount of benefits based on a percentage of their pay. This avoids the possibility of the plan favoring any specific employee, and therefore violating the rules for qualified plans. Limitations for participation in a SEP IRA cannot be stricter than being 21 years of age, working for the employer three of the last five years, and receiving annual compensation exceeding $500.
- SIMPLE IRA – This type of plan is meant for employees that work for an employer that does not offer its own employee retirement plan. It does this by allowing employees to set up a traditional IRA plan for themselves. Unlike traditional IRA plans, the SIMPLE plan allows higher contribution limits to compensate the employee for a lack of an employer plan. In 2012, the contribution limits for a SIMPLE IRA are $11,500 annually with catch-up contributions increasing the limit to $14,000 for individuals over 50.
- Solo 401(k) – Also called individual 401(k) s, these plans

operate much like a regular 401(k) plan, which will be discussed at length shortly. Solo 401(k) s are strictly for sole proprietors with no employees, however a spouse of a sole proprietor may also contribute to the plan. The plan allows the same contribution limits as a 401(k) and is also offered in both traditional and Roth format, just like an IRA. However, unlike other individual plans such as SEP IRAs, solo 401(k) s allow the owner to take loans out of the plan, just like a regular 401(k).

- 403(b) Plan – Also known as tax-sheltered annuities, a 403(b) plan is available for public school employees, tax-exempt or non-profit organizations, and religious organizations. Investment options in these plans are normally limited and conservative; mainly allowing investment in products such as mutual funds. A 403(b) plan participant can make $17,000 in contributions to the plan every year (or 20,000 if over 50) and the annual employer and employee contributions cannot exceed $50,000 or 100% or the employee's includable compensation.

- 457 Plan – A 457 plan is a retirement plan available to the employees of state and federal government agencies. A 457 plan is tax deferred but does not have matching employee contributions. A participant may defer their salary into the plan like any other retirement plan and distributions may begin at retirement age.

401(k) s

All of these plans have their place and are used when someone's specific needs require them. However, many of these plans borrow from, or are remarkably similar to, the most common defined contribution retirement plan: the 401(k). The 401(k) is a qualified plan which means that the money put in the plan is tax deferred. In 2012, the IRS increased the contribution limit to all types of 401(k) s to $17,000, up from $16,500 in 2011. They also increased the catch-up

◀ **THE RETIREMENT PITFALL**

clause for anyone over 50 to $5,500 in 2011 and 2012.[2] 401(k) s are wildly popular and come in many different varieties. However, these different 401(k) s are mainly a concern for the employers offering the plans and are not important for our purposes here.

CONTRIBUTIONS

For the employee, you must use the 401(k) plan that has been chosen for you, but the contribution limit of $17,000 is the same for every plan. You may exceed the contribution limit in a given year with an after-tax contribution, but after the limit the money in the plan will no longer be tax deductible. You will have to report that income on your tax return the year you made the contribution and the year you withdraw the money. For instance, if you exceeded the contribution limit in 2012, you would have until April 15th of 2013 to remove the money or face tax on the contribution for the 2012 year and the year you take the money out of the retirement plan.

As if that were not bad enough, the earnings of a 401(k) will still be taxed as ordinary income when withdrawn as well. If you invested in a stock, the money you contribute to a normal brokerage account will be your cost basis and any gains made in this account would be considered a capital gain if held longer than a year. At the moment, the rate of tax on ordinary income is higher than the tax on capital gains. This means if you were to withdraw the same amount of earnings from both a 401(k) and a stock investment in 2012, you would pay more tax on the 401(k) earnings. So with excess contributions to a 401(k), you are taxed when the excess goes into the account, and are taxed at ordinary income rates when you take the money out of the account. Avoid over contributing to your 401(k) at all costs! Please note, the present tax situation is not set in stone and this scenario may not always be true. Tax rates do fluctuate. In fact, the capital gains rate is going from 15% to 20% at the end of 2012, unless the government changes the law or extends the current tax rates.

Regardless of how you feel the future of tax law is going or how much you are presently putting into your 401(k), you should always find out how much your employer contributes to your 401(k). Most plans will match up to a percentage of your income or will match a certain amount of cents on every dollar you put in. You may not be able to reach your contribution limits in your 401(k), but you should try your hardest to match your employer's matching contributions for every dollar they offer.

The Roth 401(k): The New Kid on the Block

Since 2006 the Roth 401(k) has become a more and more popular employer sponsored retirement plan. The Roth 401(k) is based on the same premise as a Roth IRA: tax free growth potential. The difference between a traditional 401(k) and a Roth 401(k) is that the traditional plan has your money grow tax deferred while in the plan and is taxed as you withdraw from the plan during retirement. The Roth 401(k) uses after tax contributions to fund the plan but the earnings in the plan grow tax free. If you are concerned that you will continue to be in a high tax bracket during retirement, the tax free growth a Roth 401(k) can be an excellent feature.

Withdrawals from a Roth 401(k) should be tax free because you paid tax while contributing to the account, but the rules for your 401(k) and Roth plan still apply. You must wait at least 5 years to make any withdrawals from the plan and you will incur a 10% penalty if you attempt to withdraw from the plan before the age of 59 ½ regardless of the amount of time you have had the plan.

One of the best things about Roth 401(k) plans is that while Roth IRAs do have income restrictions, Roth 401(k) s do not. In 2012, if you claim more than $125,000 in income when filing as an individual or $183,000 when filing jointly you cannot make an Roth IRA contribution that year. Even if you're under the earnings limits, you may still only make an annual Roth IRA contribution of $5,000 a year or $6,000 for those who are over 50. The Roth 401(k), on the other hand, does not have any income restrictions on it; it must only adhere to typical 401(k) regulations, and the contribution limit for a Roth 401(k) is much higher than that of a Roth IRA. In 2012, you may

◄ **THE RETIREMENT PITFALL**

contribute up to $17,000 to your Roth 401(k). You may contribute the full amount allowable by law every year regardless of how much you claim in taxes.

Though tax-free earnings on your investments do <u>seem</u> like an excellent proposition, Roth 401(k) s may not be good for everyone. If you think you are going to be in a lower tax bracket in retirement a Roth 401(k) may not be advantageous for you. People that expect lower tax brackets after retirement will be better off with an investment like a traditional IRA that allows tax deferred growth up until taking money from the account. Also, unlike Roth IRA plans, you must begin taking distributions from your Roth 401(k) plan at age 70 ½.

On the other hand, if you expect your taxes to increase after retirement then a Roth 401(k) plan is the way to go because you can take from it without raising your taxable income. Also, a Roth 401(k) plan may benefit people that are young and can expect their income to be much higher in the future. If you are paying 20% tax when you are young, chances are you will be paying more when you are getting paid better later in life. Use your low tax bracket now to pay taxes rather than waiting for it to go up later on.

The problem with all tax advantaged plans is that the future is uncertain and it is not clear whether you will pay more tax now or more tax in retirement. The best you can do is to select the best plan based on your current situation and your expected future. Be sure to determine all aspects of your finances in order to make an informed decision.

USING AND MISUSING YOUR 401(K)

A 401(k) can be a huge asset if you use it correctly; especially if your employer is matching your contributions. Wonderful things can come from owning one, but there are also some horror stories about what people have done with them as well. There are certain things you need to be aware of when owning a 401(k).

- <u>Try to max out your 401(k)</u> – A 401(k) is a wonderful way to

RETIREMENT PLANS/IRAS

save money if you are still working. As mentioned earlier, the limit in 2012 of annual contributions is $17,000. If you are 50 or older the additional allowable catch-up contributions are $5,500. That means you can put away $22,500 every year. That is a lot of money if you ask me. If you can't make the maximum contribution, don't sweat it. Not many people do. A definite goal that you should have is to get your contribution up to your employer's matching limit. This is a must do for 401(k) owners. Matching contributions are free money with no catch. Take advantage of it.

Please note that 401(k) contribution limits apply to the sum of all your 401(k) s, both Roth 401(k), and traditional 401(k) contributions put together. You cannot put $17,000 in both a Roth 401(k) and a Traditional 401(k). The sum of the accounts may not exceed $17,000; or $22,500 for those over 50 and younger than 59 ½.

- <u>Cashing out your 401(k)</u> - Please do not do this if not absolutely necessary. A move like this could have serious negative consequences on your retirement plans. Money should only be taken out of your 401(k) for retirement purposes except for in the most extreme of circumstances. This is not "I need an extra car" money. The consequences of accessing your 401(k) before 59 ½ are numerous and very detrimental to your overall wealth. First, when you take money out of your 401(k) before 59 ½ you will be slapped with a 10% withdrawal penalty, and this is on top of your holdings being taxed at ordinary income rates. Assume you are in the 25% tax bracket, if you withdraw $100,000, you will be hit with a 10% penalty ($10,000) and then an additional 25% will be taken in income taxes ($25,000) this leaves you with only $65,000 of your original $100,000. This is a sure way to erase any gains you have made in your portfolio and then some.

Normally most businesses only allow withdrawals from a 401(k) if you are in financial hardship. You should only borrow

◄ **THE RETIREMENT PITFALL**

out of your 401(k) if you are in serious financial need or you are sure you will be able to replace the money quickly. Times have been tough recently, resulting in more 401(k) loans and withdrawals. According to data from Fidelity Investments, as recently as 2010 workers borrowing from retirement accounts was at a ten year high, with one in four workers, 22 percent of the workforce, taking out loans against their 401(k) plans. In the second quarter of 2010, 62,000 workers initiated hardship withdrawals. 45 percent of those surveyed who made hardship withdrawals in 2009, made one in 2010 as well.[3] Things may be hard, but you should only withdraw from your 401(k) if you must. Even if you really are in a tight spot, there are only certain situations where you will be allowed to withdraw money from your 401(k).

In order to obtain a 401(k) hardship withdrawal you must show that you were in immediate and heavy financial need and there are few exemptions that will forgive the 10% penalty. Employee death, employee permanent disability, separation from the job on or after the age of 55, deductible medical expenses, or a qualified domestic relations order are pretty much the only situations where the IRS shows mercy. With so few options, you must be very careful using money meant for retirement.

- Borrowing from your 401(k) - When you borrow money from your plan you must pay back that loan with interest. You may borrow up to $50,000 or 50% of the value of your plan, whichever is less. You may only borrow from your 401k only if your employer's plan allows it, but must be repaid within 5 years unless the loan was used to buy your home. Loans from your 401(k) are not subject to income tax or the 10% withdrawal fee.

However, there are other problems with taking a 401(k) loan. For instance, you probably should keep your job while you have a 401(k) loan outstanding. If you are retiring, you

RETIREMENT PLANS/IRAS

should not borrow from your 401(k) because you would have to pay that loan back soon after leaving. If you are fired or quit with an outstanding 401(k) loan it will typically have to be repaid within 60 days. If you default on a 401(k) loan the balance will be reported to the IRS and you will have to pay both the 10% withdrawal penalty and your ordinary income tax rate. These occurrences could be devastating to anyone's bottom line. Also, if the loan is preventing you from continuing to contribute to your 401(k) that can hurt your retirement as well. Some plans may actually prevent you from contributing to you plan until the loan is repaid. So, while better than an outright distribution from a 401(k), a loan is also a dangerous proposition.

Finally, for every moment that you have a loan out on your 401(k), you are missing out on possible appreciation for that portion of your savings. Do not borrow money out of your 401(k) unless there is no other viable alternative.

OTHER TIPS FOR 401(K) S:

- Review your account and rebalance the amounts of different investments you have in your 401(k) from time to time. Letting one area of the account become too large could change the risk in your account. Make a plan and stick to it.
- If you have a highly appreciated stock in your 401(k) you may not want to roll over the stock into an IRA plan to preserve the stock's net unrealized appreciation. This concept will be explained in more detail later in this chapter.
- Do not stop investing in your account. Allowing your account to flounder can have lasting consequences.
- By law, your 401(k) account will go to your spouse if you suddenly meet your demise unless you specifically state otherwise. If you would like to have another beneficiary other than your spouse, it is important to talk to your human resources department about changing the beneficiary on your

◄ THE RETIREMENT PITFALL

401(k) account. If you did not change the beneficiary on your account and there is no spouse, some accounts will send your 401(k) to a child or other relative. However, some do not, and others may have limitations on stretching and splitting the account. If your plan is inflexible, make sure that your beneficiaries know to have the 401(k) account transferred to an inherited IRA in the event that you die unexpectedly. This way the account can be stretched and split as they like.

The IRA

Qualified plans are great when you are working, but you also need a way to manage your retirement funds after you stop working. That's where personal retirement plans come in. These plans are used by people during and after their working career and are common tools in retirement planning. People use a number of ways to save and invest their money in retirement. However, by far the most commonly used retirement plan is the IRA. Therefore, it would be appropriate to cover IRAs thoroughly so when you do use an IRA, you will know how to use it more effectively and significantly improve your retirement plan.

Think of retirement plans like IRAs as a piece of complicated technology such as a computer. Many people may have a computer but few use their computer to its absolute full potential. The same could be said for how many people treat their retirement plans and their potential to maximize its benefits. Many people have them but are not truly using them in the best way possible. Educate yourself to maximize the potential of your IRA.

THE BASICS

The Traditional IRA was created under the Tax Reform Act of 1986 to give people that do not work for large corporations the opportunity to create a retirement account for themselves. IRA means Individual Retirement Account and the biggest incentive of the traditional IRA is its tax deferred status, which means the account is funded with dollars that have not been taxed. As we have discussed earlier, in 2012 the contribution limit to an IRA is $5,000 (or $6,000 if you are over 50).

If you exceed contribution limits for your IRA you may be subject to a 6% excess tax for every year you have the excess contribution in the account, regardless of whether you made a profit or not.[5] If you made a contribution of $6,000 to your IRA plan and were not over the age of 50, you exceeded your annual contributions by $1,000. This excess contribution will be taxed 6% or $60 in this scenario. If you do over contribute to your plan, you can still avoid the excess tax by withdrawing the excess amount along with any earnings the excess made by your annual tax deadline. The IRS then treats your taxes as if the excess contribution was never made.

Like other retirement plans, you may begin taking withdrawals from your account at age 59 ½ and you must take Required Minimum Distributions from the account by age 70 ½. But when you do begin taking RMDs you do not have to take the RMDs equally from each account. If you prefer one account over another you may drain the weaker account and allow the other IRA to grow until the inferior one is depleted. However, splitting your IRA does not allow you to contribute more than a total of $5,000 to all your IRAs. This means if you have 3 IRAs you are not allowed to contribute $15,000; you may only split $5,000 for all the accounts.

Rollovers

One thing that people often make mistakes on is when they are transferring assets from their other accounts into their IRAs. Often, when most people stop working at a company and begin their retirement, they feel that their money will be fine staying in their company account; which is usually a 401(k). Under certain circumstances they may be right. Employee plans do have certain perks in retirement. For instance, you may borrow against most company plans. This allows you to use the money that you have in the plan without getting taxed for it, provided that you pay it back, of course. Some plans also allow you to buy life insurance through their plan which could be much

◄ THE RETIREMENT PITFALL

easier than buying your own, especially if you are not in the best of health. Additionally, if you retire young it may be better to leave your money in your company account. If you leave a company before 59 ½, money left in a company retirement account may be accessed at age 55 if it remains in the company retirement account. After 59 ½, you can move the money however you want because you can access the money without penalty.

Want to avoid RMDs from your IRAs? Some employee plans allow you to postpone Required Minimum Distributions past age 70 ½ if you are still working with the company. However, IRA plans do not allow you to do this at all. If you do find yourself in a situation where delaying your RMDs would be advantageous and you are still working at a company where you have a qualified plan, see if it would be possible to roll your IRA over into your qualified plan in order to avoid having to pay RMDs. This tactic can make your eventual IRA payouts larger by delaying payments. Please note, not all qualified plans allow you to delay RMDs and some plans will not accept IRA rollovers. Please speak with your company before you take this plan under consideration.

WHY IRAS CAN BE BETTER THAN QUALIFIED PLANS

In most circumstances, it would probably be best to move your money into an IRA. IRAs are far more versatile than most company retirement plans. For instance, the federal government allows all IRAs to be stretched and split in any way that the owner of the plan likes. Most qualified plans, on the other hand, do not. This is not to say that the plan cannot allow for it, it's just that companies don't have to offer this in their plans, so they avoid the extra work. Stretching a qualified plan would mean that the company would have to deal with the children or grandchildren of the plan's owner. Don't count on your company wanting to do this. Besides, an IRA must do this already, so why try and reinvent the wheel?

The fact is employee plans do not want to deal with you or your beneficiaries after you have retired. Because of this, most plans are

RETIREMENT PLANS/IRAS

set up for very simple distribution methods like spousal transfers and lump sum distributions. These simple plans can hurt you in the long run. For instance, if you have an employee plan where your spouse is the beneficiary (as most plans are designated) if the spouse dies before the holder of the employee plan does, then the plan normally gives the account to a non-spouse. Since employee plans do not allow you to "stretch" the account, this means that the account will be given to the designated beneficiary in a lump sum distribution. This would cause all taxes on the account to be activated and would likely put you in a much more expensive tax bracket.

The reason that so many people roll their retirement savings over into an IRA is its ability to remain tax deferred. But if you are a 401(k) owner or the owner of another qualified plan there are restrictions on your IRAs:

- <u>You may not be able to deduct any contributions to your IRA.</u> You are already taking advantage of tax deferred savings in your 401(k) so you are gradually fazed out of this IRA perk the higher your income is. This amount varies depending on whether your filing status is married filing jointly, single, or married filing separately. For example, in 2012 if you are single the phase out for deductions begins at $56,000 and you are completely excluded at $66,000, but if you are married filing jointly the phase out begins at $110,000 and you are completely excluded at $125,000 in income.[5]
- <u>You may not be able to claim IRA deductions if your spouse is covered by a qualified plan, even if you're not covered by an employee plan.</u> You begin being phased out at $173,000 and are completely excluded from deductions at $183,000 if your spouse is covered by an employee plan.[5]
- <u>If you have no retirement plan, you may deduct the maximum amount allowed by law ($5,000 or $6,000 if you are over 50).</u> If you are married you may contribute $10,000 for both you and your spouse, but the money must be put in two separate $5,000 accounts.

◄ THE RETIREMENT PITFALL

Once the 401(k) is closed, you are free to begin making tax deferred contributions to your IRA again. You are allowed larger tax deferred contributions under a 401(k); however, retirees are unable to take advantage of this perk. When you retire from your job you will be unable to contribute to your company's 401(k). This is because you can only contribute money you earned from that company to fund the company 401(k).

Once you have retired, it is probably better to roll your 401(k) over into an IRA because with an IRA you can use any earned income to make a contribution. For instance, if you are working a part time job after you retire, you would not be able to contribute that money to your 401(k), but you would certainly be able to put that money into your IRA. If you want to continue to save in retirement an IRA clearly has its advantages.

IRAs can also be more versatile compared to an employer sponsored account. In an IRA account, the account is merely a vehicle. Unlike most employee plans were the investments are controlled by an account manager for the fund or mandated through some sort of policy; With IRAs, the investor can open an account and invest in almost anything they like. I know that sometimes too many options can be overwhelming, and that too much information is certainly a possibility in the financial services industry, but more choices also mean more control of your destiny. With IRAs you can control what investments your money goes to.

IRAs may also be easier to use than other retirement plans. When you are in a 401(k) plan you have to work through an intermediary to get access to your money. In circumstances like withdrawals, you must ask the plan permission to take the withdrawal. This could involve a considerable amount of time and paperwork to get access to your money and you shouldn't have to ask permission to get your own money. With an IRA, you are the only one that needs to sign anything to get access to your money. The process is streamlined and the paperwork is less than you would normally find with a 401(k). If you are looking for choice, access, and convenience as a retiree IRAs

RETIREMENT PLANS/IRAS

are typically easier than qualified plans.

One misconception that I commonly hear concerning IRAs and 401(k)s is that IRAs have fees where as 401(k)s do not. With a 401(k), the fees may not be on your statement, but make no mistake there are fees with every retirement product. No one works for free. The custodian of your 401(k) account must get paid for their work on your retirement plan. With a 401(k) the fee is simply absorbed into the cost of maintaining the account and is not directly reported to you. IRAs are more straightforward and tell you what the plan is costing you. Don't be fooled into thinking that anyone would not charge you for their services. All plans get paid somehow.

IRAs can also simplify your investment records. IRAs allow multiple investments to be rolled over into them, allowing you to have one place to go to keep track of your investments while still maintaining your tax deferred status. Fewer investment accounts mean less paperwork and a more complete understanding of your net worth. Please consult your taxation and financial professionals before you combine investments just to be perfectly sure there will be no negative consequences in doing so.

Ultimately, IRAs give you tax deferred savings of your retirement money and many more choices concerning your investments. IRAs also give you the ability to contribute to the dynasty that you are attempting to build and gives your family members a legacy that will impact their lives far beyond your years. One of the most important ways IRAs can do this is by performing the wealth saving and wealth extending stretch to beneficiaries. This can extend the life of your investments far beyond your death and lead to a future of wealth and comfort in your family. But before we start talking about stretching your IRA, let's discuss how to properly rollover an existing account into an IRA.

PERFORMING THE ROLLOVER

If you do choose to rollover your qualified employee plan, there some basic rollover rules that should not be ignored.

THE RETIREMENT PITFALL

- <u>Move the Money in 60 Days</u> – When you decide to rollover an employee account into an IRA there are two ways to do it. A direct rollover will send money from one account to the other without the money being given to you. The other way to move your money is an indirect rollover where you receive a check for the funds in your account addressed to you. If you receive a check addressed to you, you have 60 days to get that money to the new account or the IRS will consider you to have collected the money and will tax the amount you received as ordinary income. This could be a massive mistake. Do not allow this to happen. Be hyper-vigilant of getting your retirement money from one account to the next.
- <u>If Possible Make a Direct Rollover</u> – If you take a rollover payment from your pension or employee plan and pay it to yourself instead of another trustee, the payor must take 20% of the value of the withdrawal for withholding. This is the way the government makes sure that you will be able to pay taxes on the amount that you take from the account and don't just spend all your money in Vegas and leave nothing for Uncle Sam. The thing is you won't get that withheld money back until you file your taxes the following year. So if you then decide to roll over the entire amount, you will have to find a way to get that remaining 20% to the new trustee or risk penalties. If you don't rollover that 20% you will get hit with the 10% early withdrawal penalty if you are under 59 ½ and you will have to pay ordinary income tax on the withholding. That's a lot of wasted money.

    A direct rollover will allow you to take the full amount out of your account and transfer it to the next account without the hassle of withholding. Most direct rollovers are done from company to company, but if you get a check during a direct rollover you have to make sure the check is made out to the custodian for your new account to avoid making the transaction an indirect rollover. Most companies want you to address

RETIREMENT PLANS/IRAS

the check a certain way such as "(Company X) FBO (your name)". Each company has their little bureaucratic nuances so be sure you contact them to get the wording they prefer.

- The One Year Rule – You may not withdraw money from any IRA you own and then put it back in an IRA tax free more than once in a given year. This is to prevent people from constantly taking short term loans out of their IRAs and putting it back before their 60 day window closes. This means if you rollover money from one IRA to another IRA on April 15th 2012, you may not rollover any more money in or out of either of those IRAs until April 15th 2013. If you do withdraw money from the same IRA twice in a year, the second withdrawal will be considered a distribution and you will be taxed on it, along with early withdrawal penalties if you are under 59 ½. Please note: In circumstances where you are making a direct rollover or transfer, the one year rule does not apply. This means you may make more than one direct rollover or transfer to an account in a year. If you receive an IRA check addressed to you and then put the money back in an IRA that is when you should worry about the one year rule.
- Don't Change Assets - When rolling over assets from one retirement account to the next make sure that you do not change the form of the asset. For example, if you take cash out of a qualified plan you must put cash into the IRA account that you are rolling over into. You may not take cash out of the account, buy stocks and bonds, and then attempt to put those into the account. If you take cash out, cash must go in. If you take out stock, stock must go back in. Even if the value of the assets is the same the IRS does not allow this type of activity. If you attempt to do something like this you will be taxed on the withdrawal at ordinary income rates, and if you are under 59 ½, you will be slapped with a 10% early withdrawal penalty. Be careful how you rollover assets.
- Watch out for RMDs – If you are over 70 ½ and considering

◄ THE RETIREMENT PITFALL

rolling your IRA over, make sure that you remove your annual RMD before you rollover the account. If you rollover an account and do not remove your RMD before doing so, that RMD amount will be considered an excess contribution and you may incur penalties.

Withdrawals

If you have a qualified plan, there is always the temptation to pull that money out of the plan in a lump sum and live the high life instead of getting the money to an IRA. I urge you not to do that. If you withdraw the money and don't get it into another account within 60 days the whole amount is taxed as ordinary income and those taxes could be a considerable amount of money. Also, if you withdraw the money before you are 59 ½ not only will you be taxed but you will also incur the 10% withdrawal penalty. This is a sure fire way to kill your hard earned gains in your retirement account. Don't do it.

If you really want to withdraw money from your qualified plan before closing it a good compromise may be to take part of the money out and contribute the rest to a retirement account. Of course, you will have to pay taxes on the withdrawal, but then you can take that fantastic vacation getaway to celebrate retirement while still protecting most of your funds.

SPECIAL WITHDRAWAL CIRCUMSTANCES

There are circumstances where you can receive special tax treatment for your withdrawals from your retirement plans.

<u>Highly Appreciated Employer Stock</u>

When you leave your job it is important that you do not roll this stock over into an IRA because doing so could have serious tax consequences. It is still safe to roll everything but the stock over. In fact, you should move everything else into an IRA so it maintains its tax deferred status, but the stocks should be moved into a regular brokerage account. What you are trying to take advantage of here is the net unrealized appreciation. Net unrealized appreciation is the differ-

RETIREMENT PLANS/IRAS

ence between what you originally paid for the employee stock in the account and the value of the stock at the time you take the stock out of the employee account. When you withdraw your company stock it creates a taxable event, but the net unrealized appreciation is taxed differently.

Let me show you how this works. When you have stock in an employee plan the value of the stock at the time of deposit is recorded into the plan. This is considered the cost basis of the employee stock in your plan. If the stock grows, the additional value will not be taxed as ordinary income when you withdraw the stocks from the account; it will be taxed only when you sell the stock. To keep this perk you must take the stocks in a lump sum distribution from the employee retirement account. When you remove the employee stock from the employee account the cost basis of the stock when it entered the employee retirement account will be immediately taxable, but the net unrealized appreciation will not be taxed until you sell the stock later on. The gains in the employee stock will be taxed at the much lower capital gains rate. This is an enormous tax advantage over rolling the stock over into an IRA and paying ordinary income tax on the full stock price!

For example, let's say Mr. Smith has 1,000 shares of employee stock in his employee plan. The shares were $10 per share when they went into the account, and during the time that Mr. Smith worked at his company the stock appreciated to $30 per share. When Mr. Smith closes his employee account and moves his stocks he will have a cost basis of $10,000 taxable at ordinary income rates and a net unrealized appreciation of $20,000. If Mr. Smith sells his stock he will have to pay ordinary income tax on the $10,000 cost basis and pay long-term capital gains on the $20,000 in gains he made while working with the company.

You also have the option of allowing the stocks to grow. After you have held the stocks in the new brokerage account for over a year, any increase in value during the time the money was in the new brokerage account will be considered long term capital gains and will

THE RETIREMENT PITFALL

be taxed at the capital gains rate. If you do not wait the year to withdraw, any gains made after you retired would be considered short term capital gains and will be taxed at ordinary income rates. If you don't need the income from the stocks immediately, you could save extra tax by waiting a year to withdraw the stocks from the account, assuming the stocks appreciate.

For instance, let's say instead of selling the stocks immediately, Mr. Smith allows the stock to appreciate to $45 per share. If he sells the stock within the first 12 months after retiring he will have to pay ordinary income rates on the additional $15,000 in gains. He will also have paid ordinary income tax on the cost basis, leaving him with $25,000 taxed at ordinary income rates and $20,000 taxed at long-term capital gains rates. If he waits the full year after transferring the account he will pay long term capital gains on both the $20,000 net unrealized appreciation and the new $15,000 gain that occurred in the new account, leaving only the original cost basis paid at ordinary income rates.

There is one last nuance to holding your stocks from an employee plan. IRS rules state that when you die holding stock that was in an employee plan, your beneficiaries will receive the same tax treatment as you did when you held the shares. This means you may have locked in the capital gains tax for the net unrealized appreciation when you withdrew your stocks from your employee account, but your beneficiaries can still enjoy what is called a stepped up basis on the rest of the account. Basically a stepped up basis eliminates the need for your beneficiaries to pay tax on anything considered to be part of that stepped up basis. This is because the stepped up basis is considered the new market value of the stock at the time of your death. In a normal stock account, the stepped up basis would kick in when you die and the beneficiaries would get the stock tax free, but that is not the case if the stock has been in an employee plan.

Let's try and explain this scenario with an example of a stepped up basis and what happens if someone dies without selling their employee stock. Let's assume Mr. Smith dies without selling 1,000 shares of employee stock and at his death the stock is valued at $30 per share. His beneficiaries would still have to pay tax on the $20,000 of the net unrealized appreciation and would not pay tax on the original $10,000 cost basis due to the stepped up basis. However, if the stock appreciated after Mr. Smith retired then that new gain would be added to the stepped up basis after his death. For instance, if the stock had appreciated to $45 per share when Mr. Smith died, the total value of the stock would be $45,000. The beneficiaries would still owe long term capital gains tax on the $20,000 of net unrealized appreciation, but the $15,000 in gains after Mr. Smith retired would be added to the stepped up basis for the beneficiaries. This means the beneficiaries would receive $25,000 of the total $45,000 tax free.

Be aware, if you decide to roll your employee stock over into an IRA, the entire amount of the stock, including any gains at any point, would be taxable as ordinary income as it is pulled out of the account by either you or your beneficiaries. Therefore, though your beneficiaries may still have to pay the long term capital gains for the increase in value during the time the stock was in your employee account, it is better than putting that stock into an IRA and paying full tax on the entire amount when you make withdrawals.

Moral of the story: If you roll the stocks in your employee plan over into an IRA you will lose the net unrealized appreciation you had in your employee plan and you will have to pay ordinary tax on the full value of the stock when you withdraw the funds. This can have a murderous tax impact on your retirement portfolio if the stock has appreciated considerably.

<u>Substantially Equal Periodic Payments (SEPPs) and Rule 72(t)</u>

For some it is necessary to get money quickly right before you reach age 59 ½ and you must begin pulling money from your IRA. Sometimes it was your plan all along and you are ready to retire early with your money. Sometimes unforeseeable circumstances force you to make a withdrawal. For those that want their retirement money early there is a way to get it, and that way is a SEPP, or a Rule 72(t). Rule 72(t) allows you to avoid the 10% penalty you are hit with for withdrawing from your retirement accounts early, given certain cir-

◄ **THE RETIREMENT PITFALL**

cumstances of course. The catch of Rule 72(t) is that once you enact the provision, you must make at least (5) Substantially Equal Periodic Payments (SEPPs) in order to avoid the 10% early withdrawal penalty. The distribution must be over a period of 5 years or until you reach the age of 59 ½, whichever comes later, and you must take this payment at least once every year. This means if you are 52 years old and begin taking SEPPs, you may not stop making withdrawals at age 57. You must continue to take SEPPs until you reach age 59 ½, which would make for a total withdrawal period of 7 ½ years. If you are 57 when you begin SEPPs, you may not stop making withdrawals at age 59 ½, you must continue the withdrawals until age 62 to avoid the 10% penalty on all of your withdrawals.

The 72(t) is not a tax free withdrawal. You will still pay ordinary earned income tax on the amount taken from the account. This is just a way to avoid the penalties involved in most early withdrawals from retirement plans. Your payments are determined using IRS actuarial calculations and the IRS takes these numbers very seriously. If you deviate from the allowed payment, higher or lower, the IRA will assess the 10% penalty to every withdrawal you have made plus interest. Make sure you have your numbers right! Investors who choose this strategy should also take into consideration the possibility of depleting their retirement account well before the end of their life expectancy.

The 72(t) plan is normally for people that retire early and need access to their IRA right away. If you retire at age 55 or older, most 401(k) plans allow you to pull from their plans penalty free so see if that is an option before you resort to the 72(t). The reason for this is if you make a mistake in making withdrawals under Rule 72(t) it could result in serious tax penalties, while the 401(k) is much more forgiving. There are calculators online that will help you determine Rule 72(t) distribution numbers if you are curious.

Stretch IRA

Now it's time for the stretch IRA, the strategy that can promote a legacy of wealth for your family. Unlike other items we have talked

RETIREMENT PLANS/IRAS

about in this chapter, the stretch IRA is not a product or investment; it is a concept. It is a way to use an IRA to extend family wealth and avoid time consuming and costly probate proceedings on your wealth when you pass on. Stretching an IRA just allows an IRA to keep doing what it does best long after you have died; which is to provide a solid tax deferred growth vehicle for your assets.

Stretch IRAs are for retirees with IRAs that do not plan on spending the entire amount of money they have accumulated in the account by the time they die. You can stretch an account by naming someone young as a beneficiary and "stretching" the Required Minimum Distributions you have over the course of their life. As per U.S. law, an IRA owner is typically required to make Required Minimum Distributions from their IRA accounts by age 70 ½. These distributions are calculated by life expectancy tables the IRS uses and the purpose of this law is to prevent people from holding onto prodigious amounts of wealth in IRA accounts where the federal government can't tax it. However, recent tax revisions have lessened the amount required in annual RMDs, which has aided in the popularity of stretch IRAs.

Though the government requires that the RMDs begin when the original owner reaches 70 ½, IRAs can be passed down from generation to generation and entirely skip the probate process, which is where many investments are killed by tax and legal fees. Also, the schedule the RMDs follow in a stretch IRA is not based on the life expectancy of the original owner of the account. It is based on the life expectancy of the person in possession of the account. This means, if given to a very young person, the RMDs required to be taken out of the account annually can be quite small. So small, in fact, that the account may still be able to make gains even when it is making RMDs. This is the reason why the stretch IRA is so popular. It makes it possible to extend family wealth far beyond your lifetime while incurring little tax intrusion from the federal government.

Most people that own an IRA typically name their spouse as their primary beneficiary and their children as contingent beneficiaries, however this may not be an effective way to "stretch" an IRA account.

◀ THE RETIREMENT PITFALL

If you die and give your IRA to your spouse the RMDs on the account are not likely to change much, assuming your spouse is a similar age to you. This will force your spouse to take large chunks of the IRA out in RMDs every year which will quickly drain the account. If your spouse does not need the money a better strategy may be to name someone much younger, such as a grandchild, as the beneficiary of the account to keep the RMDs to a minimum. The younger the child is the better as this keeps RMDs as low as possible, which can let the IRA account keep growing.

For example, if Mr. Smith died and had named his grandchild Jane (age 5) as his primary beneficiary, it is likely that Jane's life expectancy would be in excess of 75 years. To calculate Jane's RMD for that year you would take the value of the account on December 31st of the previous year and simply divide by the life expectancy of Jane. Obviously the longer your life expectancy, the lower that RMD will be. The following year you would do the same calculation with Jane's new life expectancy and the new account value to calculate the RMD for that year. This would continue until the beneficiaries life expectancy is up.

Unfortunately, this stretch concept is not allowed to go to infinity. Second generation beneficiaries do not have the ability to stretch an account. If the primary beneficiary dies and leaves the account with a second generation beneficiary, the new beneficiary would not be permitted to stretch the account to their own life expectancy. The account will still be subject to the primary beneficiary's schedule and will exhaust itself when the primary beneficiaries' life expectancy is up, despite the fact that they have already died.

Even though you cannot renew the life expectancy table for your second beneficiary, it is very important that the original beneficiary of your account be allowed to name their own beneficiary to preserve the stretch benefit you have created. If the custodian of the account does not allow your beneficiary to name their own beneficiary, then the IRA will go through probate when the original beneficiary dies and the stretch benefits will be destroyed.

RETITREMENT PLANS/IRAS

A Roth IRA can be stretched as well; unfortunately the government covered all its bases on the Roth IRA. If you have a Roth IRA you do not have to take RMDs from the account. For people that plan on keeping their IRA to pass on to their beneficiaries this is a great way to avoid tax, but this perk is only true for the owner of the account. Once the beneficiary gets the account, they will be forced to take RMDs. Roth IRAs have many advantages, but eternally preventing RMDs is not one of them.

The most apparent objective of a stretch plan would be long term tax deferral for a traditional IRA and long term tax free growth if you are stretching a Roth IRA. By stretching the account and taking less money out each year you are allowing the effect of compounding to grow your wealth. However, there are other advantages for the stretch IRA, such as the ability to avoid a big tax bill. The more income you claim in a year, the larger percentage the U.S. government will claim in tax. By stretching your IRA account you are spreading out the withdrawals of your IRA money, and therefore keeping your income in a manageable tax bracket. This can save you thousands in the long run. Another plus for stretching an IRA is that the plan can be changed if circumstances change. You must take the RMDs as a beneficiary, but you may also take more money from the account if you desire. This way if your family were to run into some difficult times your IRA could be of assistance to them.

If you have multiple beneficiaries that you want to stretch an IRA to, make sure you split the account so that each beneficiary has an IRA and name one beneficiary to each account. Then the RMDs in each IRA will pan out according to the beneficiary's individual life expectancy. If you do not split the account, then the RMDs will be doled out according to the eldest grandchild's life expectancy. If there is a large gap in age between the grandchildren, this could have a significant impact on the long term growth of the IRA account, and the account may not last for the youngest grandchild.

There can be down sides to the stretch IRA. For one, once you pass away and bequeath the account to your beneficiary you have no

◄ THE RETIREMENT PITFALL

control over the account. Also, the beneficiary of the account is not subject to the early withdrawal penalties that you had to deal with. After you pass the government wants its money and is going to make it easy for your beneficiary to get to it. The idea may be to secure your grandson's future, but he or she may want a Lamborghini. It is important that you stress the purpose of the account to your beneficiaries. If the account is large and only RMDs are taken, it could single handedly secure the retirement of your grandchildren. Make sure they know that.

One thing that you must remember is that things change and you may want to rethink your strategy on stretching out your IRA. Unless they are much younger, giving your IRA to a spouse will not result in an effective stretch policy, but when you die your spouse may need money. One way you can solve this problem is name your spouse the primary beneficiary and name someone like your grandchild the contingent beneficiary. This way, your spouse will have the ability to accept the IRA if they need the money, or they can disclaim the inheritance if they want to pass it on to your grandchild. If your spouse disclaims the IRA and it passes on to your contingent beneficiary the stretch will still take effect.

Important:
1. If you plan on stretching an IRA, make sure you have an IRA custodian that allows stretching, because not all do. It will be a disaster if you plan to stretch an IRA only to find out too late that it isn't possible with the IRA custodian you have.
2. Regardless of whether you plan on stretching your IRA or not, make sure you have a beneficiary on your IRA account. If you don't, normally you will be forced to make a lump sum distribution, which offers no benefits and will cause a taxable event for the entire account.

Stretching an IRA account can be a big decision and means that you must trust others that may not know how long you have worked for this money. However, it is an excellent way to provide an opportunity to extend your wealth to your progeny and give them opportunities you never had. Know the options your custodian gives to you before you move forward with a stretch plan and take the time to find out if a stretch IRA will work for you and your family.

Roth IRA

The Roth IRA has not been around for long, but has certainly had a significant impact on how people spend their money and save for retirement. Simply put, a Roth IRA is a retirement plan funded with after tax dollars that is permitted to grow tax free. That means that the earnings on a Roth account will never be disturbed by tax. Because Roth IRAs use after tax dollars, the government also has no incentive to force you to liquidate the account so they can collect tax. The result is an account that does not force RMDs at any time during the life of the owner. Contribution limits for Roth IRAs are the same as for traditional IRAs $5,000 per year or $6,000 if you are over 50. Additionally, unlike traditional IRAs, Roth IRA accounts have no age limits for their contributions, so you may put money into the account until you die. This can offer tremendous advantages to people that expect to have a high annual income in retirement or people that are planning on using their IRA as a gift to their heirs.

Converting to a Roth IRA

Many people do not start investing with a Roth IRA. It is often the case that they change their traditional IRA to a Roth IRA later in their careers when their retirement objectives become clearer. Consequently, it is important to know how these conversions can affect your assets.

You may convert as much money as you want from an IRA to a Roth IRA. You're taxed on the conversion so the government is perfectly happy with this arrangement. However, rather than performing a full conversion, it may be better to convert your IRA to a Roth IRA in sections to avoid climbing into the higher tax brackets.

Many mistakes are made when people attempt to convert their IRAs, and it is usually because they get caught by an IRA nuance they

◄ THE RETIREMENT PITFALL

are unaware of. After age 70 ½, the first dollars that come out of your traditional IRA every year are considered your RMDs. RMDs are not allowed to be converted into another IRA or another retirement plan, this includes Roth IRAs. This means that you must take out your RMD requirements for that year before you make a Roth conversion. Also, when performing conversions you cannot change the form of the assets. Cash must stay cash; stock must stay stock, and so on.

When you do convert a tax deferred account to a Roth IRA, you should be prepared to pay the taxes due with money that is not part of the IRA account. When you pay for the conversion with money outside the account you are keeping you are maintaining the strength of your investment while improving the purchasing power of the account in retirement. If you use money from inside the account your gains will be smaller for the same percentile gain. Also, if you are under 59 ½ you should not take funds from your IRA account to pay the taxes on a Roth IRA conversion, because if you do you'll be hit with the 10% early withdrawal fee! If you do not have the money to pay all the taxes up front on the Roth conversion, it may be better to not convert your account at all. However, if you are dead set on conversion, another option is converting the account in smaller more manageable pieces. A partial conversion will keep you in a lower tax bracket at will make the conversion taxes more manageable.

Paying for the Roth IRA conversion up front with money from savings can also save you money in the long run. Let us assume that you have an IRA that is worth $100,000 and that taxes on this account would be 30% for someone in your tax bracket. If you pay the conversion taxes from inside the account the total of the final Roth account will be $70,000. If you made a 50% gain in the account in the next 10 years, the final amount of the account would be $105,000. On the other hand, if you paid the conversion taxes with a savings account the Roth account would still be worth $100,000 after taxes. If you made a 50% gain on this account the final value of the account would be $150,000 tax free.

Some will say that you would make the same amount of money

RETIREMENT PLANS/IRAS

by letting the savings account grow alongside the Roth IRA. So let's assume you paid the conversion tax from inside the IRA account and kept the $30,000 you would have paid in tax in a savings account. If the account made a 50% gain like the other accounts it would have appreciated to $45,000. Then after you paid the 15% capital gains tax of $2,250 on the $15,000 in gains, you would be left with $42,750 total in the savings account. The after-tax savings account combined with the $105,000 Roth account is $147,750. That's less than the $150,000 you would have if you paid the Roth conversion taxes with the savings account. Thus making the outside payment of Roth conversion taxes a better investment strategy.

Do not convert to a Roth IRA if you plan on needing your money anytime soon. In addition to having to be 59 ½ to withdraw from any IRA account, when you convert a Roth IRA account you must have the account for 5 years before you can begin to access the money inside of it. If you violate the 5 year rule you'll be hit with the 10% early withdrawal penalty.

Maybe you chose to make a Roth account, but you realize you have made a mistake. Maybe you have decided in the end that the benefits of a Roth plan do not outweigh the benefits of a traditional IRA plan. Maybe you have realized that you cannot afford the taxes due on the conversion of your account. Whatever the reason, it may not be too late to get yourself out of this pickle. What you need to do is recharaterize your account, which basically means put the account back the way it was before you made the conversion. There is no penalty to do so, as long as you change the account back by the time that year's taxes are due. Also, in order to recharacterize, you must move the money in a trustee to trustee transfer. You are not permitted to rollover the account when you recharacterize.

ROTH IRA RULES

Roth IRAs follow a withdrawal scheme called FIFO(first in first out). This means that the first dollars into the account are the first dollars pulled out. In addition to FIFO, all Roth IRA accounts follow ordering rules that determine the sequence of the money coming out the account. The first money to come out of a Roth IRA when you make withdrawals will come from your contributions. Contributions are after tax money that you pay directly into a Roth IRA. Contributions are not taxed when you withdraw them and you may withdraw these funds at any time. Conversions are money that comes from traditional IRAs that you convert into Roth IRAs. To withdraw conversion money you must be either over 59 ½ or past the 5 year conversion period to avoid penalties. Gains are the last thing to come out of a Roth IRA. With gains you must be over 59 ½ and you must wait 5 years before withdrawing that money without penalties. Be sure you know what the status of your money is in your Roth IRA before you make withdrawals.

INHERITING A ROTH IRA AS A SPOUSE

If you inherit a Roth IRA as a spouse, there are certain things you must consider before you do anything to the account. A spouse has more options when inheriting any IRA, including a Roth IRA, but doing the wrong thing with the account can be costly.

If you do not choose to treat the account as your own you will be seen to have inherited the account, which will activate the Roth IRAs RMDs for beneficiaries. If you do treat the account as your own the restrictions on the account will not be based on the age of the deceased spouse, they will be based on your age. The account will assess early withdrawal penalties if you make withdrawals when you are under 59 ½, but since it is now technically your Roth IRA, RMDs will not begin during your lifetime.

ROTH? OR NO ROTH?

Though there are plenty of up-sides to Roth accounts, you may still be debating whether or not to go through with a Roth conversion. Is it better to hold on to the tax deferred money and let it grow, or pay the tax now and have my earnings grow tax free? The fact of the matter is that both IRAs and Roth IRAs have their advantages and dis-

RETIREMENT PLANS/IRAS

advantages; it really depends on what your plans are for your money and what you think the future will look like.

- <u>Do you have money available to pay the conversion charges?</u> I would recommend against converting your IRA to a Roth IRA if you don't have the cash available to pay the taxes during the conversion. If you pay tax with account funds you are depleting the power of the account.
- <u>Do you need the money soon?</u> If you need the money in the near future a Roth IRA account may not be for you. When you convert from an IRA to a Roth IRA the money in the account will be stuck there for the next 5 years unless you're willing to pay penalties. Also, by removing the money quickly, you are not allowing the account to take advantage of tax free gains.
- <u>What will your taxes look like in the future?</u> If you think that taxes will increase in the future or you will be in a higher tax bracket later in life a Roth IRA could be useful. If you believe that you will be paying less tax in the future, then a traditional IRA may be better.
- <u>What is the money for?</u> One advantage of Roth IRAs is that they do not force the owner to take RMDs from the account. However, this is only an advantage if you do not plan on making withdrawals in the first place. A Roth IRA is excellent for passing money on to heirs or as an account that you will access later. If you were going to use that IRA as a source of income, the lack of RMDs will make little difference to you.

When making the transition to retirement there are many choices to make, and the options and nuances of these choices are numerous. As I'm sure you are aware, these selections are important and can have a significant impact on the health of your investments. Always fully consider your financial situation and more importantly what your objectives for your money are when choosing an appropriate retirement plan. Having knowledge of these accounts can mean the difference between retirement success and making a horrible error that could cost you thousands.

◂ THE RETIREMENT PITFALL

QUICK REFERENCE CHART: IRAs AND 401(k)s[6]

Roth 401(k) plan	Roth IRA	Traditional 401(k) plan
Employee contributions are made with *after-tax* dollars.	Same as Roth 401(k) plan.	Employee contributions are made with *before-tax* dollars.
Investment growth accumulates without any tax consequences.	Same as Roth 401(k) plan.	Investment growth is not subject to Federal and most State income taxes until funds are withdrawn.
No income limitation to participate.	Income limits: married couples, $183,000, singles, $125,000 adjusted gross income.	Same as Roth 401(k) plan. No income limitation to participate.
Contribution limited to $17,000 in 2012 ($22,500 for employees 50 or over).	Contribution limited to $5,000 in 2012 ($6,000 for employees 50 or over).	Same as Roth 401(k) plan.
Withdrawals of contributions and investment growth are not taxed provided recipient is at least age 59½ and the account is held for at least five years.	Same as Roth 401(k) plan.	Withdrawals of contributions and investment growth are subject to Federal and most State income taxes.
Distributions must begin no later than age 70½. (This may change.)	No requirement to start taking distributions.	Same as Roth 401(k) plan.

Chapter 7 Endnotes

1. "Stock Investing Advice | Stock Research." *Fool.com: Stock Investing Advice*. Web. 30 Apr. 2012. <http://www.fool.com/?source=iflsittph0000001>.
2. "IRC 401(k) Plans - Operating a 401(k) Plan." *Internal Revenue Service*. Web. 30 Apr. 2012. <http://www.irs.gov/retirement/article/0,,id=119625,00.html>.
3. GOLODRYGA, BIANNA, and JESSICA HOPPER. "Shrinking Savings: Record Number of Americans Dip Into Retirement Nest Egg." *ABC News*. ABC News Network, 20 Aug. 2010. Web. 22 Mar. 2012. <http://abcnews.go.com/WN/record-number-americans-dip-401k-retirement-accounts-loans/story?id=11448653>.
4. "What You Should Know About Your Retirement Plan." *United States Department of Labor*. Web. 01 May 2012. <http://www.dol.gov/ebsa/publications/wyskapr.html>.
5. "Amount of Roth IRA Contributions That You Can Make for 2012." *Amount of Roth IRA Contributions That You Can Make for 2012*. Web. 04 June 2012. <http://www.irs.gov/retirement/participant/article/0%2C%2Cid%3D188238%2C00.html>
6. "Another Retirement Savings Option: Roth 401(k) Plan." *U.S. Bureau of Labor Statistics*. U.S. Bureau of Labor Statistics. Web. 21 May 2012. <http://www.bls.gov/opub/cwc/cm20060221ar01p1.htm>.

CHAPTER 8

Insurance In Retirement

"Defense is superior to opulence."
– Adam Smith

BUILDING WEALTH AND accumulating a nest egg for retirement is certainly very important. People spend their entire adult lives preparing for the moment when they will have to put their money into action and start digging into their savings. But perhaps equally important is defending that money from events that would destroy even the most well planned retirement. Things such as illness and the unknown can strike without warning and need to be prepared for, but even the worst scenarios can be managed with the proper protection. This is the objective of insurance. In order to have a complete retirement plan you must have safeguards like insurance in place to prevent its destruction. This chapter is dedicated to determining which insurances are most advantageous to have as you design your retirement plans.

At their most basic level, insurance policies save you from financial ruin by spreading risk. Services like life and auto insurance allow you to do this by paying a premium to the company in return for them covering your expenses in the event of a covered loss such as death or an auto accident. The insurance company is basically playing a game of numbers, betting that terrible life events will not happen to all of its customers at the same time. If this holds true, the insurance company can pay the claims of people that do need help with the collected premiums of customers that aren't making claims.

While you are younger, you typically insure most of the things that are important in your life. The average American will have a homeowners insurance protecting against theft, accidents, and fire. They will have an automotive policy to protect them from the costs of an accident, and they will have health insurance to protect them from a medical emergency. They may also have a life insurance policy to protect their loved ones in the event of their death. All of these policies are meant to give you peace of mind knowing that one serious emergency will not destroy your entire life plan.

As you get older the needs you have and the uses you have for insurance change, and as a retiree you need to be prepared to change your policies in order to adapt. As I'm sure you know, premiums on policies such as life and health insurance increase as you age due to the increased likelihood of having a covered event occur. These rate hikes can really dig into your savings as time goes on. To make effective retirement decisions you have to reevaluate and modify your insurance policies when it is necessary.

If you are still living in a home or if you are still driving a car, it is often mandatory to have insurance policies for these items. So unless you plan on not driving or getting rid of your house, those costs must remain. To be sure, health insurance is not something that you should skimp on. As you get older the cost of health insurance does go up, but only because the chance of you getting sick increases. Because of this, health insurance is also necessary. If you get seriously ill without coverage, rest assured that not having coverage will be hideously expensive. What good is saving money if you die anyway? You need health insurance and you need to budget the money to afford it. Life insurance, on the other hand, is a variable.

Life Insurance

Do you need life insurance in your old age? Well the answer to the question depends on you. The reason that life insurance is dif-

◀ THE RETIREMENT PITFALL

ferent than the other insurances that people typically buy is that life insurance benefits other people. Other insurances such as auto, health, and homeowners typically benefit the owner of the policy. This means that life insurance may eventually lose its potency if circumstances change. Most people increase their life insurance policy when they are married, have kids, or are the only one supporting the family, but if your spouse gets a job, or if your children move out the need for a strong life insurance policy diminishes. However, despite the shrinking need of an insurance policy as you age, you may not want to cancel your policy entirely. There are still expenses that everyone must account for when they say goodbye such funeral and burial costs. A small life insurance policy could help your family pay for your final expenses.

Some people have done an excellent job planning their retirement and have accumulated so much wealth they feel that life insurance is just not worth the money. If you have designed a plan where you have constant and dependable streams of income funding your retirement, your need for life insurance may be less, but life insurance is not without its uses even for the retired wealthy. Many people use life insurance as a way to pay costly estate taxes when they die without being forced to sell the asset being taxed. The great thing about using a life insurance policy in this manner is that death benefits from life insurance policies are income tax free, so if you have a large benefit it could prove incredibly useful in paying off estate tax.

The desire to leave a legacy is another reason that someone who has a large amount of retirement savings would want a life policy. Maybe the future of your family and loved ones outweigh your needs at the moment. Maybe you just know that you have more money than you know what to do with. Regardless of your motives, it is always an option to forego a little money now to buy a life insurance policy that ensures your loved ones are comfortable when you pass.

For those of us who did not save as well as they might have wanted, life insurance can provide other perks. If you do not have a large amount of money and you are married you should be concerned

INSURANCE IN RETIREMENT

about the well being of your spouse if you were to die before them. Having a life policy to fall back on can keep them safe even when you're gone.

So the choice of whether or not to have a strong life insurance policy basically amounts to what you think is best for your family if you pass on. Some people will decide that life insurance is not necessary and some will find it indispensible. Regardless of your feelings on your situation, you should talk about this issue with your loved ones and possibly an estate lawyer. They would be able to determine the consequences of a life insurance policy on your situation and which one may be best for you.

TERM VS. PERMANENT LIFE INSURANCE

Now that you've determined if a life policy is generally right for you, let's get a bit more specific about policies. One issue that everyone has when getting life insurance is whether to get a term policy or a permanent policy.

Term insurance is to protect against some sort of risk within a specific time frame. For instance, if you have children and worry about you passing before they are grown, a term policy may be the right choice for you. The reason for this is there's a finite period of time that you are trying to cover, which is the time when your children are in your home with no other means of support but you. Eventually they will grow up, get jobs, and you will no longer have to worry about them, thus ending the need for that life insurance policy. Term insurance would also be good to use if you have a risky job or if you are in a financial agreement with someone else. If you are a stunt man or demolitions expert, term life insurance may be a good idea. Also, if you are in a business venture with another person and their death would ruin your business, it would be wise to take term insurance out on them as well.

Permanent insurance is for an indefinite risk. If you're thinking of the long term welfare of your family, then policies like whole life or universal life may be right for you. Also, if you have a large part of

◄ THE RETIREMENT PITFALL

your retirement plan contingent on your survival, then a whole life policy is an excellent choice as well. For example, say you have a pension that provides most of your retirement income. That pension is guaranteed for life... your life. If you have a spouse that also depends on that income your death could leave them out in the cold. Having a permanent policy in this scenario would be indispensible.

TYPES OF PERMANENT LIFE INSURANCE

Term insurance typically has a fairly simple format. You pay an annual premium, and for that year you receive a specific amount of coverage. Permanent insurances have many more shapes and sizes, but for the most part there are several basic formats.

- Whole Life – Whole life insurance is the most familiar type of life insurance to most people. You pay a set premium throughout your life and receive a death benefit upon your death. Whole life policies also typically have a surrender value that the life insurance company will give you if you decide to close your policy. You also may borrow against the cash value in your policy and pay it back at a later time.
- Universal Life – Universal life insurance differs from traditional whole life because the premium on the account is adjustable. Of course if you lower the premium in the account that will also lower the coverage that the insurance company gives you. The advantage of such a policy is that you may adjust the coverage in your policy based on what is happening in your life. If you have a cash value in the account you do not even need to make a payment; the insurance will use the cash value in the account to pay the premiums.
- Variable Life – A variable life insurance policy allows the investor to choose what investments the policy has. This allows the account to potentially grow quicker, but also subjects the owner of the account to investment risk. There is a guaranteed death benefit on a variable life insurance policy, but the cash value in the account is not guaranteed and could suffer from

INSURANCE IN RETIREMENT

bad investments. Also, the guaranteed death benefit is based on the claims paying ability of the issuer.

There are many choices for life insurance, but some of these choices are not appropriate for someone that is approaching retirement age. When you are about to retire your concerns are very different from someone that may just be starting out in their career or just had children. On the whole, most retirees have two major concerns that life insurance can help them with. 1. What will happen to my family if I suddenly pass away? 2. How do I protect my estate from tax? Let's look into specific policies that can help with these concerns.

SINGLE PREMIUM LIFE INSURANCE

If you have a large amount of money saved up and would like to establish a life insurance policy, it may be beneficial to establish a single premium life insurance policy. Like other life insurance policies, a single premium policy will take into account the age and health of the insured to determine the cost of the policy and the death benefit. However, single premium policies are superior to the more common gradual premium polices in that the account is immediately paid off, which then allows the whole lump sum of money in the account to grow immediately.

The reason that single premium life insurance is attractive to many retirees is that these policies have something called living benefits. That means the owner of the policy may withdraw money from the death benefit before they pass on to pay for expenses due to things like illness or long term care. However, nothing is free. When you add a livings benefits rider or get a policy that includes living benefits, you guessed it, premiums go up.

SURVIVORSHIP POLICIES

Survivorship policies have a variety of uses:
- <u>It will protect younger generations</u>. If you are concerned what will happen to your children or grandchildren in the event of you and your spouse's death, a survivorship policy can be

very effective. This way you can provide money beyond the estate that you have developed.
- It can pay estate tax. As we know, estate tax can be delayed when assets transfer from one spouse to another, and this is why paying estate tax is one of the most common uses for survivorship policies. After the second spouse dies your heirs may face a large tax bill. By having a survivorship policy you can avoid the toll estate taxes will have on your assets, thereby passing down a larger estate. If you assess the size of your estate, it should be easy to estimate the benefit needed for a survivorship policy to cover the tax on your estate.
- If your assets are illiquid a survivorship policy could be especially beneficial for you. Having to pay large estate taxes could force you to sell your illiquid assets like your house at a fraction of its real value. This may be the last thing that you want to do if you have plans for giving these assets away! Having a survivorship policy can keep your estate in one piece.
- Survivorship polices are less expensive than single-insured life insurance policies. Single life policies do pay after the death of an individual spouse, so it may be a good policy if you are worried about providing for your husband or wife when you die. However, survivorship policies are much cheaper because they pay when the 2nd spouse dies. If passing on wealth or protecting your estate is your objective, a survivorship policy may be a much better plan.
- Survivorship polices are easier to get. If you have a spouse that is not in the best of health, insurance premiums on an individual life insurance policy may be extremely high or they may be denied coverage outright. A survivorship policy is an affordable way to have an insurance policy that covers both spouses regardless of one spouse being ill.

Unwanted Policies

After a certain age and after certain life events it often becomes

INSURANCE IN RETIREMENT

less beneficial to have certain types of life insurance. If you find yourself in a position where you have a policy or policy premiums that you would rather do without, there are number of things you can do.

- <u>You could surrender the policy.</u> If you plan on surrendering your policy make sure you check with your insurance company that you will not encounter any penalties for doing so. I would only suggest surrendering a policy after you are past the surrender period for your policy to avoid penalties. Also, if you surrender your policy that may create a taxable event. Be careful not to propel yourself into a higher tax bracket by surrendering your insurance.
- <u>You could buy a smaller paid-up policy.</u> This would allow you to continue to have insurance coverage without having to pay premiums. If you are concerned about having no insurance coverage this may be an option for you.
- <u>You could sell the policy.</u> Many times selling your life insurance policy may get you more money than if you surrender the policy. This is because the insurance company does not want you to cancel the policy because they would then stop getting premiums. Consequently, they may set the surrender value lower than the cash value and the death benefit. An investor may pay you more because they are interested in buying the policy and collecting the death benefit on the policy when you pass on. Investors may be especially interested in taking your policy off your hands if you are not in the best of health. If it is more important to you to get money now than when you die, then selling your policy could be an excellent choice for you.

Long Term Care

One of the most important insurances to consider when you are planning your retirement is the long term care policy. All too often, this insurance is overlooked by retirees who end up paying thousands upon thousands down the road in costs for things like nursing homes or at home care. The status of your health when you begin retirement can be drastically different than when you are ten or twenty years down the road. Though you may feel fine now, it is important that you use caution and take the all appropriate steps for your continued protection.

Many people do not think they need long term care insurance when they reach retirement, but the statistics prove otherwise. According to the U.S. Government, about 70% of people over age 65 will need long term care services during their lifetime and more than 40% will need care in a nursing home.[1] This means that the odds of ending up needing your long term care insurance is 70%. Doesn't it seem prudent to insure against a 70% chance of anything bad happening? Unfortunately, many long term care policies are prohibitively expensive; the average long term care policy runs between $1,000 and $3,000 annually.[2] However, this is nothing compared to paying for your nursing home costs out of pocket. It is important that you find efficient ways to afford this care. We will discuss ways to make long term care affordable later in the chapter.

Though most people do end up needing long term care, there are risk factors to help you determine whether you should get a policy if you are undecided.

- Gender – Whether you are a man or a woman could be important when deciding if you need long term care. Women typically live longer than men and tend to be by themselves in the later stages of life. They therefore run a higher risk of needing long term care.
- Family – If you have a large family with the resources to take care of you in your old age it may not be necessary to have long term care. However, you never know how things are going to turn out. Be careful when asking family to take on such an enormous obligation.
- Health History – Does a chronic or debilitating disease run in your family? It may be hard to think about, but if that's the case you should definitely consider getting a long term care

INSURANCE IN RETIREMENT

policy so you can get the care you need if you are suddenly stricken.
- Life Expectancy – If your family has a tendency to live long, you may want to consider the need for long term care. The longer you live the more likely it is you will need it.

Take inventory of all the factors that would suggest the need for a long term care policy. It is also important to remember that the unexpected happens and spending a couple thousand a year in insurance is far better than losing your life savings paying for care.

TYPES OF LONG TERM CARE

Just like any type of insurance there are many options available for long term care that fit many different needs. Qualified long term care policies typically require that:
1. Care is expected for at least 90 days.
2. That person cannot perform at least 2 activities of daily living such as dressing, bathing, toileting, eating, transferring, or continence (or) there is a need for assistance due to mental impairment.

In both cases, a doctor must provide care or a plan in order for the long term care plan to be considered qualified. The benefit of having a qualified long term care plan is that the benefits of the plan are not taxable.

Types of Plans
- Reimbursement Long Term Care – Reimbursement policies are the most common type of polices sold. These policies typically cover your expenses on a daily, weekly, or monthly basis up to a certain amount. After this amount you are on your own affording the additional cost. The insurer may pay these costs directly or you may be reimbursed by the insurer at a later time, but they will only pay for the cost of the long term care. The remainder of your daily benefits will stay in a pool to extend your benefits later on. For example, if you had a policy that had $100,000 in benefits, this policy may have

a daily benefit cap of $100. This means that if you took the maximum benefit every day the policy would last for 1,000 days. However, if you needed $70 a day for care, the policy would pay you the $70 you need and put the $30 you didn't need in a pool. The policy would then allow you to take from the pool until you reach your overall benefit limit.

- Indemnity Long Term Care – In an indemnity plan, when you claim benefits the insurance policy pays you the entire daily benefit every day regardless of the cost of the care. For example, if you had a policy that had a daily benefit limit of $100 but the care you are receiving costs $70. The plan would still pay you the full $100 and you could pocket the extra $30. Due to this, these policies tend to be more expensive than the reimbursement policies.
- CASH Plans - Some indemnity plans known as CASH plans will pay your benefit regardless of whether or not you use a licensed care giver or nursing home. All that it requires is that you prove the loss of two activities of daily living or the loss of cognitive impairment and you then qualify for benefits. Of course, this perk makes the premiums on the policy higher than most other plans.
- Partnership Long Term Care – Partnership long term care is designed to offer people an incentive to use long term care before they resort to using Medicaid. Under normal circumstances, people are only allowed to apply for Medicaid when they are legally destitute. Under a partnership program, if you use up all your long term care and do end up needing Medicaid, the program will ignore your assets by the amount of long term care coverage you have purchased; thereby allowing you to get Medicaid while still having money to your name. For example, if you buy a policy that has a $200,000 benefit limit, if you are part of a partnership program, $200,000 of your assets will be saved from being collected by Medicaid. In order to be part of a partnership plan the long term care plan you

INSURANCE IN RETIREMENT

have must be a tax qualified plan, the plan must have inflation protection, and partnership plans must be offered in your state.

Most long term care policies have daily benefits somewhere between $50 and $300. The per-diem benefit will typically buy you decent long term care coverage today, but not necessarily tomorrow. Because of this, most policies now offer inflation adjustments in order to keep your daily benefits comparable to the actual cost of care when you need it. Many policies will simply increase the benefit amount every year by a specified percentage to keep pace with inflation. Be aware that with long term care polices, the at home care daily limit is normally smaller than the nursing home daily limit and that any expenses over the daily limit that you have, you are responsible for. Take into account the policy you can afford and the level of care you would like to receive when shopping for a long term care policy.

SELECTING THE RIGHT LTC POLICY

Often with long term care polices, many of the mistakes made are due to unfamiliarity with what the costly parts of long term care are. People often cover care for nursing homes assuming that an overnight facility would be the most costly form of care, but this is normally not the case. At a facility, you are going to the nurses; with at home care, the nurses are coming to you. Also, if you require 24 hour care that means that the caretakers are billing you on a 24 hour basis. According to the Department of Health and Human Services, in 2009 the average cost for home care was $21 an hour. Twenty-one dollars an hour for 24 hours is $504 a day. That will erode your savings quickly. Whenever you are buying insurance, it is always best to cover the worst possible situations first. This way you will not be bankrupted by a horrible catastrophe. Since at home care can be more expensive and is commonly less covered in long term care policies, give special attention to that matter when choosing your long term care polices and riders.

Also, most long term care polices have elimination periods on them. Most of them are about 90 days long. Some policies even require that this elimination period restart every time that you reenter a nursing facility or apply for care. Paying for 90 days of long term care before your policy kicks in can be extremely expensive, especially if you make multiple visits to the facility, thus restarting the elimination period each time. Make sure you have a way of paying for these first 90 days or find a way to shorten the elimination period on your long term care policy. Be aware, more often than not, Medicare will not provide coverage in long term care situations.

Reading your policy thoroughly is very important as well. The fine print in long term care polices can be very important. One thing you should pay special attention to is what the policy considers an "activity of daily living". Almost all long term care policies will pay benefits if you cannot perform two actives of daily living or are cognitively impaired. Most policies consider bathing, grooming, clothing, continence, toileting, transference, and ambulation as activities of daily living. However this is not guaranteed. You do not want to find out later when you lose your ability to walk that it is not considered an activity of daily living by your long term care policy. Also, be sure you are completely clear on the limits of the policy. Some policies have limits paid by the day, others pay by the week, and some pay by the month. Not understanding how your policy pays out or the amount of coverage that you have can have serious consequences. Be sure that you understand the policy completely and that it covers things that are important to your standard of living. Some polices have language that is complex and industry specific. It would be best to have someone versed in this contract language explain the policy to you so that there is no confusion as to what you are buying.

Should You Get Long Term Care Insurance?

Many people ask me if there are any alternatives to long term care. There are, but they may not match up to the benefits of long term care insurance. One of the few viable alternatives to long term care is setting up a fund that you will be able to call upon if long term care is needed, but that is much easier said than done. Growing a fund to the size that would be needed to handle the expense of long term care would take a lot of time and money. Many middle class Americans will not have the money to get a fund like this to the point where it will cover the costs of long term care. With insurance you will have money guaranteed up to the cap on the policy, regardless of your savings or the performance of your investments.

Waiting to get a long term care policy is also likely a bad idea. The older you are the more expensive premiums in a long term care policy will be, so if you want a policy get it now. In addition, and probably more importantly, if you wait too long you may make yourself uninsurable. Almost all long term care policies will want to cover a 55 year old healthy man, but many will think twice before insuring a 75 year old with a chronic illness, don't put yourself in that unfortunate position.

What If You Don't Get Long Term Care?

Healthcare in America is one of the best programs in the developed world. However, the success of the program is also turning into its greatest challenge. Many people are living much longer and living through increasingly dangerous diseases and operations. Many people believe that their health insurance will take care of any health problems that they have. However, most health insurance is designed to treat patients quickly and release them. Normal health insurance is not designed to cover long term handicaps and chronic conditions. As you age, the likelihood of having such a condition gets larger and the result is that many more people are in need of long term care. However, many people either do not understand they need coverage, or choose not to get coverage because they cannot pay for it. What they do not realize is that they will either pay a little now or pay a lot later. As we have discussed earlier, the annual cost of a long term care policy is between $1,000 and $3,000 per year and about 70% of people will at some point need long term care. In contrast, a one bedroom unit in an assisted living facility averages about $3,131 per

◄ **THE RETIREMENT PITFALL**

month.³ If you must use a long term care facility when uninsured, those insurance premiums will quickly seem like small potatoes.

<u>Will Medicare Pay?</u>

Long term care is expensive, and you will likely need it, so finding a way to afford long term care could mean the difference between options and treatment in difficult times or seeing your life savings slip away. Unfortunately, long term care is not covered in normal health policies and it seems that the U.S. government is largely unwilling to cover long term care costs through Medicare. After a hospital stay of 3 days and nights Medicare will cover part of a stay in a skilled nursing facility for 100 days. However, Medicare is extremely specific about what they mean when they say this. For instance, if you stay in a hospital 3 days and 2 nights you will not be covered for your subsequent skilled nursing stay in any facility. If you are not getting "skilled nursing" care you will not be covered. A vast majority of the time, care given in a long term care facility such as a nursing home is not considered skilled care and will not be covered by Medicare. Also, any custodial care will not be covered by Medicare. So if you have someone taking care of your home during at home care, that service will not be covered. Even if you are deemed to be receiving skilled care, you typically must be making rehabilitative progress to remain on Medicare, and once you pass the 100 days of care you are cut off from Medicare coverage.

<u>What About Medicaid?</u>

If Medicare does not work out you may turn to Medicaid. However, having to turn to Medicaid can be frightening. Medicaid will normally only take patients if you can prove you are legally destitute. The requirements are different from state to state, but it generally means that the person receiving care has almost nothing to their name other than a car and a home. The Medicaid program will take everything else to help pay for the care the state will give you. Obviously, this will destroy your estate and almost any hope of passing wealth on to heirs. In addition, once you are part of the Medicaid program, you have very little choice in what facilities you may use, and the facili-

INSURANCE IN RETIREMENT

ties available often do not offer the level of care that a private nursing facility would.

It is very important that you take time to think about the consequences of not having a long term care policy. Paying now may be difficult, but always consider the options available for those that choose to have a long term care plan and the options for those that choose not to pay. Take care now to have a solid plan in place for the years you may not be able to care for yourself.

Making Long Term Care Affordable

Despite long term care being expensive, the cost is not set in stone. There are a number of ways to get the cost of a long term care policy down. Some of which will have a significant impact on the overall cost of the policy.

- Pay your premium once annually. Whenever you pay insurance premiums once annually you are saving the insurance company time and processing costs. Insurance companies will normally offer discounts to people who will pay their annual premiums in total because of this.
- Increase your elimination period. Long term care polices work a lot like health insurance and deductibles in this respect. With health insurance, the larger your deductible is the less your premium will be. With long term care insurance, the longer the elimination period the less your premium will be.
- Get a group discount. If you work for a company that offers long term care, it may be better to get a policy through them and take advantage of the lower rates group policies enjoy. Be careful when getting these polices though. Sometimes the benefits in group polices are inferior to the benefits you get with an individual policy.
- Get a tax deduction. If your policy is expensive, it may be possible to use that to your advantage. Long term care policies are considered medical expenses. The IRS stipulates that anyone who has medical expenses that exceed 7.5% of your

gross income may claim the excess expense as a deduction. It can be difficult for 7.5% of your gross income to go to medical expenses, but if this is the case, make sure you get that deduction!

- Stay Healthy. If you are in good health that's fantastic. Make sure you stay that way by going to the gym, eating smart, and avoiding smoking. Long term care policies take into account your past health history and current health condition. Staying in good health will allow you to get a good rate.
- Get a spousal discount. Having you and your spouse on the same plan can provide a discount for the both of you. You both need the insurance so why not?
- Buy your insurance policy early. Premiums are mainly based on age so the earlier you buy a long term care policy; the cheaper the policy will be in the long run. In the case of long term care, it does not pay to wait and buy a policy. Assuming you buy inflation protection and your health remains constant, if you buy a policy at 55 the total premiums you pay will likely be smaller and the overall benefit will likely be larger than someone who buys the same policy at 75. You could pay less and get more in 30 years than someone who pays for the same policy for 10 years simply because you started earlier. Deals like this do not come along every day.

Many people believe that the money they spend on long term care insurance is wasted if they do not end up using their policy. However, as with all insurance, long term care insurance is a way to be safe rather than sorry. People buy insurance all the time and don't use it. That's how insurance companies stay in business. Do you buy car insurance and get mad when you don't get into an accident? Do you buy health insurance and hope to fall ill? Do you buy homeowners insurance and hope a natural disaster happens? Of course you don't. Your attitude about long term care insurance should be the same.

Insurance can be used for many things throughout your life, but in retirement the game changes slightly. It is even more important to have the correct insurance after you retire because your income is generally fixed. In the past if you suffered some uninsured catastrophe there was always a way to make that money back through working. In retirement this is no longer an option. The specter of illness and tax on your assets can crumble even the most well planned nest eggs. Make sure you have the proper insurances for your situation to defend yourself from the unknown. Buying insurance is not wasting money; buying insurance is paying for peace of mind.

CHAPTER 8 ENDNOTES

1. U.S. Department of Health and Human Services, National Clearinghouse for Long-Term Care Information, <http://www.longtermcare.gov/LTC/Main_Site/Understanding/Definition/Know.aspx> Web. 14 May 2012.
2. "Eight Ways To Save On Long Term Care Insurance Premiums." *Long Term Care Insurance Premiums*. Web. 14 May 2012. <http://www.completelongtermcare.com/resources/how-to-save.aspx>.
3. "KHN: Kaiser Health News." *Few Seniors Have Long-Term Care Insurance*. Web. 15 May 2012. <http://www.kaiserhealthnews.org/features/insuring-your-health/michelle-andrews-on-long-term-care-policies.aspx>.

CHAPTER 9

Estate Planning

"A life lived for others, is the only life worth living."
  – Abraham Lincoln

MOST OF LIFE involves making things go well for yourself, but once you have done this, it becomes important to turn your attention to other things. As you age, you begin to realize that part of your duty is to provide security for your family's future. A way to provide that security is to offer what you have earned in your life to strengthen and secure your family as a whole. This is where your estate comes in. Some retirees will be able to wield great power with their assets even after they pass; some will leave a more modest imprint. However, even the largest estate can be reduced to rubble if the estate is not well planned. I have seen millions of dollars of hard earned investments be lost to the heavy effects of estate tax, poor management of assets, and the squabbling of heirs. This chapter will discuss the ways to avoid common estate problems and how to build an estate that is sure to have an impact.

What is Estate Planning?

Some people will try to make estates sound like very complex things that most people know little about, but in reality they are a very simple concept. An estate is everything you own. This would include things such as cash and banks accounts, investments, businesses, real

ESTATE PLANNING

estate, retirement plans, and benefits from life insurance policies if they are paid to your estate. Surprisingly, people often under appraise the value of their estate.

Regardless of the size, it is still important to protect the things that you have from what happens to your estate when you die. Having a plan to protect your assets gives you a number of benefits that you will not have with your estate otherwise. Among other things, estate planning gives you the ability to name your heirs and make legally binding wishes for your assets, plan an efficient way to pay or even avoid estate tax, and prevent conflicts over your possessions after you pass. Good estate planning should also include what will happen if you suddenly become incapacitated. It could be disastrous if something horribly unfortunate happens to you and you are unable to make important decisions without a properly planned estate.

Without an estate plan, it is not uncommon for the government to take control of your assets. The government's plan is just what you would expect if a stranger was given complete control of your wealth; it keeps a lot for itself. Without a planned estate the government may also be forced to make medical decisions for you. No one wants that! Having estate documents such as a will allows you to avoid losing control after you die and prevents the government from stepping in and using their plan. Don't let all of your wealth go wasted. Allow your heirs to enjoy your legacy by passing your possessions on to them.

Estate plans typically have some key items that make them strong and effective. We will get into more forms of these items later in the chapter, but a brief list of these items would include:
- A Will
- A Living Will
- A Power of Attorney
- Trusts

Some people will need all of these items and some people may need a more simple solution for their estate, but all can play an important part in a proper estate. Everyone's needs are different and different situations will be identified later to help you best match your needs with an appropriate strategy.

Few people really enjoy estate planning. It is a morbid task, but it is something that you must do. The consequences of not completing a plan are many and costly. If you have put estate planning off until this point it is imperative that you begin right away. Make the tough decisions today so that your family can have peace of mind when you pass on.

What Do You Have?

Before we get into the types of estate plans, we need to know what it is that we are working with. When planning an estate, one of the first things you should attempt to do is determine where all of your assets are and how much they are worth. The chapter in this book on financial planning will help you brainstorm on how to assess your full net worth, but put simply, your taxable estate is the fair market value of everything you own when you die. This sum is essentially everything that will be able to settle any debts you have at the time of your death. Things such as taxes, outstanding debts from creditors, and funeral expenses will be deducted from the estate until they are all paid off. Then the estate will be distributed to the heirs of the estate according to your will, or the government plan if you have no will.

After you assess the value of your estate it is important to know if you fall into the group that would have to file an estate tax return. The Tax Relief Act of 2001 reduced the estate and gift tax rates from 55% in 2001 to 35% in 2012, and has slowly raised the estate tax exemption over the last ten years. In 2012 you do not have to file an estate tax return unless the total value of your estate exceeds $5,120,000. The estate tax filing limit has been rising steadily throughout the 2000s, but the future of the estate tax exemption is in question. If the current laws are allowed to lapse, the result will be a return to a 55% estate tax or higher, and the plummeting of the exemption for filing and estate tax return from $5.12 million to $1 million. If you are planning an estate, it would be best to keep your eye on the outcome of this legislative issue.

ESTATE PLANNING

Common Estate Plans

Once you have found the value of your estate, you must then make a decision as to how you are going to pass this money on. This is the primary task of an estate plan. There are many ways to pass your wealth on, but most people stick to a couple methods that tend to cover the vast majority of estate planning situations. This section will detail these plans so you can see which will best fit your needs.

Wills

Regardless of your wishes, every estate should at least begin with a will. This is because a will tells everyone what it is you want done with your estate and where things should go when you die. A will does have its drawbacks, which we will discuss, but it is far better than dying intestate. Intestacy laws are different from state to state, but generally speaking, the state will divide your assets between a surviving spouse and your children. If you die with no children then the state will decide which of your heirs will get your inheritance. Dying intestate leaves no directions for your estate and will surely create chaos after you pass.

When constructing a will you must make sure your assets are in order and then decide what you want to do with them, but be careful how you make these decisions. You must find people who are trustworthy enough to take care of your finances and business affairs when you pass and must decide who will make medical decisions in the event that you are unable to make them for yourself. Most importantly, you must decide who will inherit your assets. After you make these decisions, it is often best not to leave those who are involved in the decision in the dark until the will is read after you say goodbye, especially if the bequeathing is in any way surprising. That's a sure way to start a battle over your estate. The more honest you are about your will, the more likely it will be that people will respect your wishes when the will takes effect. It will also allow your heirs to ask questions and discuss your decisions and may save your wishes from being misunderstood.

◂ THE RETIREMENT PITFALL

A will can work in tandem with other parts of your retirement as well. Without other documents to assist your will there may be confusion during probate and then who knows what the court will end up ruling. Any change to your will needs to be followed up on to make sure all details are taken care of. In addition to your will, you may want to have a trust in place to add detail to your wishes. Trusts can be used to enhance wills by putting conditions on the money and assets that you bequeath after you die. They also offer an opportunity to avoid estate tax if used correctly. Trusts are not a substitute for a will because, while a will attempts to cover the totality of your estate, trusts often deal with a specific piece of property or a specific wish that you have.

Wills do have their weak spots. For example, wills will only control assets that are specifically in your name. That means if you have an asset that is jointly owned by both you and your spouse, those assets will be excluded from your will. Also, many retirement assets such as IRAs and life insurance policies have beneficiary designations. This means that they skip probate, but it also means that your will does not have control of those assets. These assets will automatically pass to the beneficiary you name on the account upon your death, regardless of what is stated in your will.

The assets that your will does control will be subject to a process called probate. Probate is a legal proceeding that determines if your will is valid, that your debts are paid before the assets of the estate are distributed, and that your will is followed appropriately. Probate completes this process by temporarily taking control of your estate, meaning you lose control. For instance, if you did not change the title on assets that are named in your will, the only legal way to change the title if you are unable to sign is through probate. This means that if you die, your family or friends cannot change your assets for you, only the probate court can. On top of losing control of the estate, all of these legal changes and proceedings are going to be very expensive. There will be various court and legal fees that will pile on top of any debts and taxes that you have on your estate, further eroding your

ESTATE PLANNING

wealth. Probate can also be a lengthy process, sometimes lasting a year or two. If you need assets immediately after someone passes, the time period where the estate's assets are frozen in probate can have a terrible effect on the well being of everyone involved.

Another drawback of the probate process is that it is completely public. Any party interested in knowing the proceedings of the process, including the value of the estate, can go find out whatever they want. Even people that you may want to keep away from the estate can take a look. There are companies and solicitors out there that use probate proceedings as a way to gather information. If they find that your family has a considerable estate, rest assured the calls will begin. This open aspect of probate may also encourage challenges to the will from heirs unhappy with what they discover. This can result in further loses through legal costs and a lengthy extension of the proceedings.

Many people think that if their will is strong then their estate planning is complete, but I have seen many challenges to wills during probate destroy what once was a strong will, and a happy family. Many people also believe that if their will's method of distribution is easy or simple, there will be no challenges to the will, but things can go very wrong during probate very easily.

In one family I have worked with there was a mother, a son, and a daughter. Sadly, the mother had become very ill toward the end of her life. The family did not want to send her to a nursing home, thinking that a loved one would provide better care for her, so the daughter stepped in to provide assistance. The demands of her care were so great that the daughter was forced to quit a very lucrative job to give her mother full time care. About three years after the mother fell ill she died. The will that was left for the estate said that all assets that the mother had should be split evenly between the son and daughter. However, the daughter challenged the will. In light of the last three years of continual care that she provided her mother, she felt that she was entitled to more than half. She had to make many personal sacrifices, quit her job where she was making

◄ THE RETIREMENT PITFALL

over $100,000 per year, and slowly see her mother slip away. The case can definitely be made that she deserved more than half of her mother's assets upon her death. However, the son believed that the will should stand as is and that each of them is entitled to half of the estate. What followed was an intense legal battle for the estate that seemed only to pay the lawyers. By the end, the estate was a fraction of what it used to be, to the point of almost not being worth fighting for. But the worst part is that the last time I spoke to the daughter she said that she would never talk to her brother again. By the look on her face, I could see that she was not joking. It is very important that you make an estate that is beyond reproach in order to prevent even the possibility of this happening. Instead of blaming each other, they may blame you, but then the blame will be buried with you and they will still have each other.

When planning an estate, the probate process is something that you would likely want to avoid. However, if you are incapacitated and not killed, your possessions will not enter probate, but your will cannot take effect. Unless otherwise stated, the court will appoint someone to take care of the decisions involving your welfare.

One way to avoid having the court appoint a guardian if you are incapacitated is by constructing a living will. A living will lets people know what you want if you are still alive but unable to make decisions. For instance, living wills typically include what you would like doctors and hospitals to do if you are in a coma, on life support, or have some sort of terminal disease. These decisions may be hard to make about your own health, but it will save your family the additional stress of deciding what to do if you are ever in this sort of situation. Your family might argue with each other about what you might have wanted forever, but if you expressly state your wishes the chances for opposition are slim. Chances are that your heirs will abide by your living will, but in some states a living will does not have to be followed. If you really want to make sure that your health wishes are followed then you could write up an advance directive for health care. An advance directive gives legal authority to someone to

ESTATE PLANNING

make decisions if you are unable to do so. There is no argument with a document like that.

Another common solution to the issue of decision making when dealing with incapacity is the durable power of attorney. While the living will and advance healthcare directive deal with your medical needs, a durable power of attorney allows someone to act as your fiduciary. This means they must manage your life business while you are unable to and act in your best financial interests. A durable power of attorney becomes effective immediately after you sign your papers and the person you deem your agent does not need to prove that you are incapacitated in order to sign your name. The more prudent type of power of attorney that is typically used in estate planning is called the springing power of attorney. With this power of attorney, a specific event, such as incapacity, must occur in order for your chosen agent to act on your behalf. This may be a safer way to grant decision making power if you feel that a durable power of attorney may be abused in some way. You may choose a friend or family member when picking an agent or you may pick an outside party such as a bank or a lawyer. Typically friends and family won't require compensation for this responsibility, but often others will. If you choose an outside party, be prepared for their bill as well. This is still better than not having an appointed agent and having the court appoint one; one you possibly may not have wanted at all.

A power of attorney will normally resolve the issues involving incapacity, but in some circumstances they won't. Some financial institutions are very cautious when dealing with a durable power of attorney, and some institutions will only take a durable power of attorney that has been made out on their forms. They do not want the liability of mistakenly handing your assets over to someone that does not have proper authorization, so normally they are ultra cautious when it comes to this. Make sure your financial organizations are comfortable handing over your assets to wherever you want them to go.

The inability to control assets during incapacity can have disastrous consequences if you do not plan properly. If you are in-

◄ THE RETIREMENT PITFALL

capacitated normally your medical bills will be astoundingly high. This may cause the need to come up with some quick cash to pay for expenses. However, your family would not be able to sell your assets if the titles to these assets are in your name. This can put a serious strain on your family as they try to come up with the money and may be forced to hand your assets over to the courts so that they can distribute funds as needed. This can be both costly and time consuming.

Finally, if you have children, they will not be allowed to take possession of any willed assets until they reach the age of majority and the court will be forced to appoint a guardian that will control the assets until then. This means that money essentially disappears until the child is 18. Many people think that if they have their will create a trust it will allow the family to take control of the assets until the child is older. However, if the trust is created by your will then the trust must go through probate and your family will not have control of the money until the probate process is over. Also, the trust will not be activated if you are incapacitated because it is part of your will, and therefore the trust does not exist until you are deceased.

At this point it should be clear that sometimes even an elaborate will is not enough for a strong estate plan. Other things are needed to manage, protect, and distribute your wealth when you pass on. Thankfully, there are ways that this can be done.

GIVING IT ALL AWAY

In order to avoid estate tax some people attempt to have as little as possible in their name before they pass away. However, there are a number of problems with this estate planning theory. First off, it's not possible to accurately predict when you are going to die. If you give all your assets away and live for another 5 years are you going to live in abject poverty? You may think that you are able to depend on the good will of the people that you are giving the money to, but it is best to be careful. Now that they have your wealth, are you sure they will give you everything you need? There is always the possibility they will lose possession of the money as well. Are you willing to take that

ESTATE PLANNING

chance? Giving your money away can be quite the gamble.

Also the government is wise to your game and has set up laws and taxes that prevent you from easily passing assets from one family member to the next. Anytime you give more than $13,000 annually to a person you must file a gift-tax return that will count toward your lifetime estate tax exclusion. That means if you exceed the $13,000 limit on individual gifts, the amount that you exceed the limit by will be subtracted from your estate tax exemption limit of $5,120,000. So if you exceed the gift tax limit by $120,000 then the maximum exemption you can claim for your estate when you die is $5,000,000. In 2012, if you exceed the total exclusion throughout your life you will be hit with a 35% tax on any gifts exceeding that amount and if Congress does not act by the end of 2012, that gift tax rate could jump to 55%.

The U.S. government has also enacted laws that prevent you from dwindling your estate right before you die to get below the estate tax exemption level. Any gift that you make in the last three years of your life does not detract from your total estate value, thereby making gifts on your deathbed still taxable to your estate.

However, there are safe ways to give your money away.
- In 2012, the gift limit is $13,000. You may give $13,000 a year to as many people as you like without penalty. If you are married you may combine both of your gift limits and give $26,000 to any individual.
- You may give money over the gift limit without incurring any taxes. You may pay an unlimited amount of medical or education bills for the people you love, as long as you pay the bills directly.
- You may exceed the annual $13,000 limit in gifts to make a contribution to a 529 education savings plan. These contributions are considered gifts but you may make one large $65,000 payment if you are single or one $130,000 payment if you are married. You will not be able to make any more contributions for 5 years because the contribution will be

THE RETIREMENT PITFALL

treated as five years of $13,000 payments, but it will not be seen as exceeding the gift limit. If you die before the end of this 5-year period, only the years you were alive will be subtracted from your taxable estate. For example if you lived two years of the 5-year period and donated $65,000, $26,000 will be subtracted from your estate. The rest of the gift is still considered part of your estate and can be taxed.

- There is also the option of donating money to charities. Charitable gift funds allow you to make tax exempt contributions to a fund that you may gift to a charity at anytime, thereby shrinking your estate. There are also investments like the charitable remainder trust that allows you to kill two birds with one stone by building a fund that gives the principal to a charity while giving the interest gained on the trust to your heirs.

Giving money away can shrink your estate, but there may be unintended consequences for the beneficiaries of your gifts. Transferring property while you are alive is different than transferring property after you die because there are different tax consequences. For instance, let's assume Mr. Smith has owned a house for the last 30 years. When he bought the house, he paid $50,000 for it. The house has now appreciated to $300,000. Mr. Smith then gave the house away to his son John, who sold the house for $300,000. Because Mr. Smith gave the house away while he was living, the cost basis that will be used to assess capital gains on the property will be $50,000, the value of the house when Mr. Smith bought the house. The appreciation of the house will be treated as a capital gain, and in 2012 that would trigger a tax bill of $37,500.

If Mr. Smith had waited to give the house to his son until after he died, the tax situation would be completely different. Because the house is then considered an inheritance, the value of the house at the time John receives it is considered the new stepped up basis. This means that if John were to sell the house after Mr. Smith's death, the $300,000 sale would be completely tax free. So while giving assets

ESTATE PLANNING

away does shrink your estate and avoid tax, be careful that you are not inadvertently putting your tax burden on your loved ones.

JOINT OWNERSHIP

When you marry, more often than not, the property you owned individually is now owned jointly with your spouse. From bank accounts to houses, most people that are married do own things jointly. Joint ownership essentially means that when the first spouse dies the second spouse will immediately take possession of the deceased spouse's assets, and the assets transferred to the surviving spouse will avoid probate. However, this does not make joint ownership an very effective estate planning tool. For instance, when the surviving spouse dies probate will take place on both spouses' assets, which will enact probate fees and estate taxes. In essence, joint ownership is just delaying the inevitable and only provides probate free transfers for the surviving spouse. With families that have children this should come as little comfort because your estate will go through probate as it passes to them.

Even more concerning should be how easy it is to disinherit children under joint ownership. If you die and the surviving spouse remarries that opens up a whole new can of worms. For example, let's say there is a couple Mr. and Mrs. Smith who have three children. If Mr. Smith dies all of his assets will transfer to Mrs. Smith under a joint ownership. If Mrs. Smith remarries to Mr. Anderson she may choose to take joint ownership of her possessions with Mr. Anderson. If Mrs. Smith then dies, all of her possessions will then be the property of Mr. Anderson. Mr. Anderson then has absolutely no responsibility to pay anything to the Smith children. Even if Mrs. Smith had willed her things to her children, if they are jointly owned, then they will pass to the surviving spouse and the will means nothing.

Joint ownership may also be used for people outside of a marriage too. The most common type of joint ownership outside of marriage is between a parent and a child. However, this arrangement has dangers that you must be aware of even if the child you are entering into joint ownership with is financially stable.

THE RETIREMENT PITFALL

- If your child is not an only child it may be a mistake entering into a joint ownership situation with them. For instance, let's say you have three children but you own your home jointly with one of them. Even though your will may say that you want your property split evenly between all of the siblings, the joint ownership will override your will and the house will pass directly to the one child upon your death, leaving the others with nothing.
- What if your son gets a divorce? Any property that you and your son own jointly may be claimed by the ex-spouse. This can be especially bad if you joint own your home with your child. If the ex-spouse claims the house as an asset that means if you want to take out a loan on the house or sell the house, the ex-spouse will have to sign off on the transaction. They can hold off on doing what you want for any reason whatsoever, which can make your life extremely difficult.
- Any trouble that you child gets into may become your problem as well. If the child that you own joint property with is involved in some sort of lawsuit, you may quickly get pulled into legal trouble. Also, if your joint owner is in money trouble, the property you jointly own is fair game to be taken away to settle his or her debts. Additionally, if either you or your child becomes ill and is uninsured or hospitalized, creditors can collect on the jointly owned property, which could put the other healthy party in serious financial trouble.

If you have to own property jointly, make sure the person that you are sharing possessions with is good with money, because it could mean bad news for you if they are careless. Finally, be careful who you share property with because it could be difficult to change your mind. There is no guarantee that everything will always go well with your joint owner. Getting someone's name off of something that is jointly owned is tough and will likely end in a legal dispute.

BENEFICIARY TRANSFERS

Many investment plans now have beneficiary designations where the assets will directly transfer to the beneficiary upon your death. These plans have the advantage of avoiding probate and are fairly simple procedures. However, problems occur when your plan does not follow what happens in life. If the beneficiary of the account is incapacitated when you die, the court will take control of those funds for them. If they die before you or at the same time, the account will have to go through probate. If you do not name a specific beneficiary or sign the account over to your estate then the court will have to determine who to distribute the money to and the asset will likely go through probate. Also, if you have a beneficiary that is a minor when you pass away, the courts will likely get involved because large payments to a minor need proper management.

If your beneficiary is your spouse it would be wise to name a contingent beneficiary so the account does not get pushed into probate if the two of you are in an unfortunate accident. Protect your estate by being prepared for whatever life throws your way.

Trusts

Many estate tools have their shortfalls, but many of these shortfalls can be corrected by a trust. Trusts can be the answer to many estate planning issues because they allow you to keep control of assets even after you have said goodbye.

Types of Trust

There are many types of trusts that do various things to help make your estate more successful. Let's review some standard types of trusts to see how they can meet the different needs of estate planning.

- <u>Revocable Living Trust</u> – This trust plan is commonly used for estate planning. Unlike a will, revocable living trusts allow you to avoid costly probate proceedings, control your assets and prevent the court from getting your assets if you are incapacitated. The idea behind a revocable living trust is to give your possessions over to the trust so that you are no longer in control of those items. Because you are no longer controlling

◄ THE RETIREMENT PITFALL

the items, this means that they avoid probate. However, assets that are in a living trust are still part of your estate and therefore may be subject to estate tax.

Legally speaking, you have changed the title on your assets in a revocable living trust and do not posses them, but essentially you are still in control of your assets. You may sell your assets and buy more assets to add to the trust. You may even cancel a revocable living trust if you feel there is a better way to estate plan. You may even have more control than you did before, because the interesting thing about a trust is that even after you die you do not lose control of the items in the trust. The instructions in your living trust will survive you and will pay your beneficiaries according to the conditions you specify being met, providing excellent control of your assets. A living trust must be well executed to work effectively. Make sure the details are taken care of in order to ensure proper use of your living trust.

- Irrevocable Trust – As a rule, trusts that are revocable remain part of your estate even though they are in a trust. This means when you pass on those trusts will be subject to tax. However, once you place an asset in an irrevocable trust you lose control of the item but it is exempt from estate tax. Because irrevocable trusts are considered to not be part of your estate they can be an extremely useful estate planning tool. People will often put life insurance policies in these irrevocable trusts to avoid estate tax on the large death benefits. Death benefits from life insurance are already income tax free but not estate tax free if held in your name. If the insurance policy is held in an irrevocable trust all proceeds can be completely tax free of both types of tax.
- Dynasty Trust – Also known as a generation-skipping trust. This trust allows you to transfer money tax free to beneficiaries that are at least two generations your junior. This type of trust is typically used to give money to grandchildren because

ESTATE PLANNING

that avoids taxes that result from giving money directly to your children. Your kids are not left out entirely either. They can receive proceeds from the earnings in the trust; the trust just cannot be in their name.

- <u>Credit Shelter Trust</u> – Also known as a bypass trust. When using this trust people will write a will that bequeaths money to the bypass trust up to the estate tax limit and then passes the rest of their money to their spouse tax free. The primary reason people do this is because putting the money in the trust allows you to use the federal government's estate tax exemption twice. For instance, if Mr. Smith had $8 million dollars and dies in 2012 he would have to pay a large amount of estate tax using his single exemption. If he wills away up to $5,120,000 to the trust and then leaves the rest to his spouse he can use his individual estate tax exemption to fund the trust and then when Mrs. Smith dies she can use her exemption to pass the rest of the money tax free.

    You can pass money to your children directly up to the estate tax exemption, but it is nice to have a trust account that your surviving spouse can call on if he or she is in financial trouble. The surviving spouse is technically the beneficiary of the trust and can take distributions from the trust when needed. The trust also keeps that money away from your children if you are worried about your heirs being too young and blowing their inheritance or abandoning your spouse if he or she needs money.

- <u>Qualified Personal Residence Trust (QPRT)</u> – This trust is meant to take the value of your home or other property out of your estate, thereby possibly avoiding tax. A QPRT lets you gift your house to your children, but you get to keep control of it for a certain period of time. The transferring of a property to a QPRT is considered a gift, but the gift is considered worth less by the IRS the longer you hold onto the house, thereby lowering your gift tax penalty. So your $500,000 house maybe be valued as a gift of $350,000 at the end of the term of the trust. The catch is if you don't outlive the trust the house will be put into your estate at full market value. If you do outlive the trust the value of gift will decrease, but you then must move out of your house or pay fair market rent to your children to continue living there. On the plus side paying rent will continue to lower the value of your estate.

- <u>The WRAP Trust</u> - A WRAP trust is an estate planning tool that allows you to put assets out of your estate while being able to access them. In order for a WRAP trust to work you must put something like a life insurance policy inside of the trust. Since the trust is irrevocable it is excluded from your estate when you die, but you may still access the cash value of the policy in the trust through loans. You may then borrow against the policy in the trust. The money you borrow from the account is paid upon your death by your estate, thereby reducing your taxable estate. Also, the death benefit is tax free because the trust is not part of your estate. For example, if you have an estate worth $7 million and you have borrowed $500,000 from your WRAP account, your estate will pay off the WRAP loan, lowering your taxable estate to $6.5 million.

- <u>Qualified Terminable Interest Property Trust (QTIP)</u> – A QTIP trust is for families that have endured a number of marriages, divorces, children and stepchildren. This trust attempts to ensure that only your children receive money and property. Your surviving spouse will receive an income from the trust and will give the principal and remainder of the trust to your named beneficiaries when you die. This means if you do not want certain children to get money, with this trust they don't have to. The down side is that this trust obviously isn't built to create harmony. It is quite possible that selectively choosing beneficiaries will destroy a family. However, if you are legitimately concerned about where your money is going, it may be necessary. Unlike a bypass trust, this trust is also part of your spouse's taxable estate and could create a considerable tax bill.

There are many more kinds of trusts available, each specifically designed to meet a certain estate planning need. Attorneys can even design a custom made trust if you feel that standard trusts do not meet your needs. As long as it's within the law, it's possible.

Funding a Trust

When you make a trust it is not enough to simply establish the trust account. You must also change the title on any account that you wish to be part of the trust. This is called funding the trust. For instance, if you have an account that is in your name, (for example: Mr. Smith) in order to include the item in the trust you will have to change the name of the account to something like "Mr. Smith, trustee of the Smith Family Trust". Any change to the trust will also have to be signed and dated by the trustee to ensure they have approved that change. So round up any bank accounts, stocks, bonds, real estate, and any other valuables that you want in the trust and make sure they are correctly named to the account.

Trustees

When choosing a trustee you will want to find someone that has the knowledge and experience in legal and financial matters to effectively control your assets. Many people prefer to use a professional trustee. Banks and trust companies that specialize in asset management are great choices for people that do not know someone that will be able to run their trust effectively. A professional trustee would also eliminate the issue of losing control of a trust because something happens to your personal trustee. Trust companies have investment managers to look after your account and make sure that your wishes are being followed. They are also government regulated to guarantee everything is being done by the book. The down side is that they will not have the personal knowledge of you and your specific situation like a personal friend, or a family member would.

If you would like to use a loved one as a trustee, there are many things to consider. Make sure they are trustworthy and have legal or financial knowledge that would make them effective. If you use a personal trustee you should have a successor trustee named that will be able to continue to control the account in the event that anything should happen to the original trustee. Also, if you have multiple children, selecting one of them as trustee over the others may begin conflicts in the family. Typically a trusted but disinterested third party serves as the best trustee.

Trust Instructions

Instructions in a trust account can be almost anything and can even be used to influence the behavior of your heirs. From distribution schedules to payments upon completion of tasks, it's all possible. For instance:

- Scheduling payments of inheritances is often used for children or grandchildren that are too young to have a sudden large inheritance because they may abuse their newfound wealth. With a trust you can be the voice of reason while still providing them with security.
- If a relative is doing work that you feel is important but does not pay well such as teaching or social work, you could instruct the trust to give them money while they perform their much needed services.
- If you have heirs that have special needs and you feel that they may not be able to handle the responsibilities of having a large amount of money at once, you may pay their rent or bills with the trust to ensure their safety.
- Even if your heirs are successful, a trust is an effective estate planning tool. Often times if you give a large inheritance outright, it may reduce the incentive for even the hardest working people to give their all. Keeping the money as scheduled payments could keep your heir's heads out of the clouds and their feet on the ground, making them productive citizens.

Keeping the money in a trust will also give the gift extra protection. Giving an heir their inheritance outright means that the money is then subject to any debts, divorces, or lawsuits that they may encounter in their life. If you hold the money in trust and pay your heirs in installments, creditors cannot touch that money to settle any issues they may have with your heirs. Also, the life events of your heirs have no impact on who possesses the money that is in your trust. If your heir gets married their new spouse has no claim to the money, if your heir gets divorced the trust is not considered their asset and their ex-spouse may not touch it. Also, if you name grandchildren as beneficiaries to your trust there is no way that they can be disinherited from the trust. The bottom line is trusts make sure that your money gets to where it's supposed to be.

Other Estate Planning Options

Although a trust is an excellent estate planning tool, it is not the only one out there. There are a number of tools you may use to get results.

Life Insurance

Permanent life insurance policies that you have held for a considerable amount of time may be a place you can go to for money by simply borrowing from the cash value of the policy. The money borrowed from the policy will be paid off by the death benefit when you pass on and the remaining death benefit will still provide money for your spouse or heirs when you die.

Life insurance is also an excellent way to protect your estate from tax. Taxes on your estate are normally due within nine months of your death, and if you're like most people you have illiquid assets such as a home, IRA, or business what will be tough to pay tax on. These taxes could result in forcing you to sell these items at a reduced price just to make tax payments. By funding a life insurance policy you can pay taxes on these assets with a modest premium payment. Also, any estate holdings over $5.12 million will have to deal with both income and estate tax. However, life insurance can be a solution to this issue. Not only will life insurance help you pay any estate tax over the exemption limit, but by paying the life insurance premiums shrinking your estate as well. If you know that your estate will exceed the estate tax limit after you die or you know that your estate will owe a large amount of income tax, having life insurance policies can cover these costs and can keep your estate whole.

If you don't want to come up with more money to fund a life insurance policy there may still be options available. Many people purchase annuities leading up to and during their life in retirement. Annuities are a great tool to provide steady income during retirement, but an unused annuity will be torn apart by taxes when you pass away. If you have an annuity that you do not need or do not plan on using during your lifetime, annuitize that account. Use the payment you receive from the annuity to fund the premium for a life insurance policy. When you die that annuity funded life insurance policy will likely provide a large income tax free death benefit that could dwarf the proceeds you would have gotten by keeping the annuity payment.

Long Term Care

Long term care insurance can be a crucial part of estate planning as well. Long term care plans are not something that you pass on to heirs, but they will protect the assets you have accumulated for retirement while you are alive. Paying nursing home costs if you are uninsured can quickly deplete your retirement savings. If you would like more information on long term care, please turn to the "Insurance in Retirement" chapter of this book.

Disclaimers

You may be undecided about who will need your inheritance when you pass on. Also, if your beneficiary is on the older side or not in the best of health, they may have estate planning on their mind. Leaving them a large inheritance could actually hurt their plans instead of lending them a hand. This is where a disclaimer will work beautifully. You can leave assets to whomever you like as a primary beneficiary, but you should also always name a contingent beneficiary. When you do that you give the primary beneficiary the opportunity to disclaim the inheritance and let it pass on to the next beneficiary. If all else fails you can always name a contingent beneficiary such as a charity if no one seems to need the inheritance. A disclaimer gives flexibility to estate plans that may be uncertain.

Making a Good Plan

When planning an estate, many people try to use the internet or legal websites that promise to give them the same results as an attorney when estate planning. The fact is they cannot give you the same help as an attorney. Legal websites let you fill out standard forms online, but they don't know you and cannot give you specific legal advice based on your situation. Remember, estate planning can involve a complex web of tax rules and regulations. Use of an experienced estate planning professional is always recommended.

Also, while there are many legal and financial steps to make a good estate plan, one part of estate planning that many people overlook is the importance of communicating the value of money with your descendants. Many families that have accumulated a vast amount of wealth fall victim to the fact that the first generation of wealthy in a family are normally very hard working and frugal, but the following generations tend to be lazy and extravagant with their spending. All your hard work building your estate will eventually be for naught if you do not make sure that your children and grandchildren respect the gift and privilege you are giving to them. Encourage your family to discuss money and how money can accomplish many things, but it cannot buy honor, integrity, and values. Teach your grandchildren how to be responsible with money through lessons in spending and simple accounting. Be honest about how you got your money and what you think the direction of your family is. Honesty and responsibility begets honesty and responsibility.

Finally, when planning your estate, always reme planning is essential for your family's future, but you Make you sure you enjoy your money as much as y

◄ THE RETIREMENT PITFALL

you decide to give it all away to your beneficiaries. Having a big bank account is nothing compared to taking a trip abroad or buying a vacation home. You earned your money, and you have to take time to enjoy it.

Epilogue

PLANNING FOR RETIREMENT is a huge commitment, but no matter what age you are it is not too late to start. Saying that you can't start a retirement account because it is too late is admitting defeat. It is never too late to get started. Overcome your fears and realize the mistakes you have made. Correct those mistakes and move on. Almost everyone that is successful has experienced many failures; those that have never experienced failure are those who have never tried.

Be smart about the way you spend and invest your money. Make sure that you recognize the aspects of your lifestyle that have been holding you back and take measures to eliminate them. Replace those vices with good habits and move in a positive direction. Don't live in a way that will hurt your future; know your financial capabilities and work within them. When you have expanded your income or increased your nest egg then you can plan how to improve your standard of living.

Make a plan and stick to it. There will be many people that will try to pull you away from your goals and what you want. However, many people don't understand how to live a financially sound life. Make sure that you don't listen to people that are offering you the easy way out. If having a successful retirement were easy, everyone would do it. Follow those who have found success in their retirement. Ask them questions and mimic what they do.

◄ THE RETIREMENT PITFALL

Don't stop learning and don't stop evaluating your progress toward your retirement. Having knowledge of what it takes to retire with security and peace of mind will lead you to where you want to be. Once you have learned, take action with what you have discovered.

I think if you take one thing from this book it should be that in order to enact change in your life you must use what you have learned. There are plenty of people that know but do not do. Have the courage to take action with your knowledge to make a better life for yourself and your loved ones. Good Luck on your journey through retirement and never forget to enjoy yourself along the way!

About the Author

Simon Chu is a Regional Vice President of **Cornerstone Financial Strategies Inc.** He has been helping mature and senior investors for many years to take control of their futures with good financial and estate planning. Simon specializes in assisting senior investors and retirees with goals such as reducing their taxable income, lowering investment risk, and increasing retirement income. He is a Certified Estate Planner, a Registered Financial Consultant and an Investment Advisor Representative with National Planning Corporation (NPC), member FINRA/SIPC.

Simon earned his Master's Degree from HOFSTRA UNIVERSITY in Long Island. He started his business career in insurance and financial services, working as a district leader with Primerica Financial Services, a member of CitiGroup. In order to help seniors more objectively to achieve their financial goals, Simon joined Cornerstone Financial Strategies Inc. and became an independent financial consultant. Simon hosts Risk Management, Retirement Investments,

◄ THE RETIREMENT PITFALL

Insurance Planning, and Estate Planning seminars for seniors, retirees, and non-profit organizations in New Jersey, New York and Pennsylvania. Simon's diverse, yet in-depth exposure to financial investment provides him with great experience and insight with investment planning, analysis, and financial decision making.

Security and Advisory Services offered through NPC, a Registered Investment Advisor. Cornerstone Financial Strategies Inc., NPC and other named entities are separate and unrelated companies.

CPSIA information can be obtained at www.ICGtesting.com
Printed in the USA
BVOW08s2031170314

347910BV00002B/123/P